C000101236

A JOURNEY INTO THE ABYSS OF THE MIND

Journey into the Abyss of the Mind
Ainsley Carter
AuthorHouse, 128 pages, (paperback) $15.18, 978-1-4772-1395-7
(Reviewed: December, 2012)

This mixed poetry and prose collection begins innocently enough with the acrostic poem "It's All About Me." Spelling the author's name vertically, the A stands for "Adorable, cute and cuddly even." Later, the S, which stands for "Sexy," hints at a bit more of what this collection makes as its central focus—the sex life and fantasies of the author.

A frequent reader of erotica will likely find many of the graphic descriptions of sex, particularly in the five short stories included here, no more inventive than the plots of storied porn movies. From a night watchman on patrol to a prisoner who escaped from jail, the stories ring familiar. Differentiating them from this genre of one-night chance encounters is the fact that nearly all of these stories end with a description of how the sex-starved couple made their encounters a regular routine.

In the poetry, the sexual language is more playful. The poems explore moments, rather than plots with a definitive end, and celebrate the object of the speaker's desires. The graphic language at times is still there, but when mixed with descriptions of a woman's "honey pot," it takes on new, and often fun, dimensions. In "The Lucky Peeping Tom," the author describes a woman as "my coco cola / Shaped woman / Tantalizing / Hot tamale / Finger licking like KFC / She meant everything to me ..." The most successful poem in the collection is one that uses this playful language that hints at attraction, only to reveal that a sleek television set was the object of the man's fantasy.

Ainsley Carter reveals a lot on the page, never shying away from feelings that are corny and romantic, as well as those that are more concerned with immediate appetites. Readers searching for a light read filled with sexual adventure may find some fun in this collection.

Also available as an ebook.

A JOURNEY INTO THE ABYSS OF THE MIND

AINSLEY CARTER

authorHOUSE®

AuthorHouse™ UK
1663 Liberty Drive
Bloomington, IN 47403 USA
www.authorhouse.co.uk
Phone: 0800.197.4150

Published by AuthorHouse   10/05/2015

ISBN: 978-1-4772-1395-7 (sc)
ISBN: 978-1-4772-1396-4 (e)

Print information available on the last page.

Any people depicted in stock imagery provided by Thinkstock are models, and such images are being used for illustrative purposes only.
Certain stock imagery © Thinkstock.

This book is printed on acid-free paper.

Because of the dynamic nature of the Internet, any web addresses or links contained in this book may have changed since publication and may no longer be valid. The views expressed in this work are solely those of the author and do not necessarily reflect the views of the publisher, and the publisher hereby disclaims any responsibility for them.

CONTENTS

BIOGRAPHY

I was born on February 6th on the Beautiful Island of Barbados, where I grew up in the parish of St George. I attained my academic education at the Workman's Primary school, then after the common entrance examination I proceeded onto The Lodge School.

Growing up in Barbados was great for me and after leaving school I chose my career path in Mental Health Nursing, which had been a great stepping stone for me. Like everything else in this world encompassed many struggles and challenges some of which left me with a bitter taste in my mouth, but none the less here I am today. Obstacles are always put in front of us to test our limits.

I remember every year when it came to having an appraisal the Ward Managers would always give me great comments, as a matter of fact almost 100% in everything from attire, personality to carrying out my work, but in the end they would always put that damper on, "Not yet ready for training", therefore I was kept back from progressing further and would sit back and watch others come way after me and would get to do their training.

However after working in the Drug Rehabilitation Unit, my then Ward manager (Group Therapist), saw my potential and backed me to go on my training (6 yrs after starting work). I was also able to attend drug seminars abroad which helped me in my field of work.

After completing my RMN studies I left Barbados behind along with a few more friends to further my career in the United Kingdom in September 2000. It was here I found my passion and love for Poetry and writing short stories.

Many days I would write and jot things down whenever I felt lonely, sad or missing family and friends and these words that I had etched on paper became my story as they had detailed my life in some way or another. Over the years I met a lot of friends here and some I allowed to peek at some of my work and most would tell me how beautiful my writing was and encourage me to publish a book, which I eventually did in September 2010, my first masterpiece called, 'Poetry a way of Life'.

Working in this field of psychiatry which deals with the mind enabled me to understand people and life much better and to actually come face to face with struggles and reasons why people do the things that they do in life, hence came the idea for my second book, 'A Journey into the Abyss of the Mind'. It comprises of Poems and a few short Erotic Stories to help ease the tension of any reader.

My Website is www.ainsleymcarter.co.uk

My LinkedIn: http://uk.linkedin.com/pub/ ainsley-carter/50/b26/840

My Blog: http://ainsleycarter-mrxqwsit. blogspot.co.uk/

ACKNOWLEDGEMENTS

My first book called 'Poetry a way of Life', has been the foundation and drive for me in completion of my second book.

My strength which pushed me onward came from God, Edmund Bradshaw (*dad*) R.I.P, Francine Carter (*mum*), Shurla Carter (*sister*), Jeron Carter (*son*), Sharon Bailey, poetic friends Carolyn 'Empresspoetry' Layne (*Author of Impressions of a Poet*), Robert Gibson, Kathy Elliot (*motivation speaker and author of many books*), upcoming Artist Shanika Thompson, Amanda Jones aka (Divinity Lace), Raylene Harris, Tammi Browne-Bannister, Cheryl Corbin, Kim N Nurse, Sean Rayside aka (*Certified Snipa*), Brantley Hunte, Hayden Shepherd, Christopher Carter, Gregory Hinds, David Griffith, Marsha Gill, Sandra Applewhaite, Adriana Alana Marion Walkes aka (*Alana Slimz*) and Franklyn Parris CEO and founder of www.Bajansunonline.com. Franklyn would always try to push me to continue my writing and has been allowing me to have space on his site to showcase and promote my work. I would also like to thank all my friends on facebook who would constantly push me and give great positive feedback and criticism about my work, without your input it would mean nothing.

Everyone has allowed me through positive and negatives to follow my dreams and make them into a reality today and I will continue to give to each and everyone more than what they expect of me and I will do this honestly and cheerfully.

My favourite quote: *Never laugh at anyone's dream: People who don't have dreams don't have much.*

PREFACE

The title of my book, 'A Journey into the Abyss of the Mind', looks at some of life's scenarios and what we as individuals are faced with on a day to day basis. Throughout this book I am hoping that the reader(s) will be able to identify with some of the struggles and understand that they are not alone and they too can shake themselves from any negativity they are faced with. *Remember after the rain always come the sun and the rainbow.*

Once I was a prisoner
In my own mind
Captured by the world of,
Greed power and crime
I have seen the world fall apart
But through poetry I shall rise . . . .
Rise above the clouds
Soaring on the winds so high
Cause this is my love, my heart
It's just the beginning . . . .
The start . . . .

INTRODUCTION

The response I had gotten from my first publication, 'Poetry a way of Life', has edged me into doing more writing and following in the footsteps of other great poets like Maya Angelou, Edgar Allan Poe, Sir Walter Raleigh etc.

I have pushed myself and was nudged along the way by my friends, Franklyn Parris and Adriana Alana Marion Walkes, aka *(Alana Slimz)* in producing this book, 'A Journey into the Abyss of the Mind'.

Along the way there was always negativity and set backs of all kinds, which in a way was good for me as I took them as they came along with the help of friends and turned them into positives. As with everything else throughout life we are all faced with struggles and problems of all types and magnitudes, but it's what we do when we confront them. Nothing in life is ever easy, as the road ahead is always long and winding, but perseverance seldom fails. Having and believing in your higher power will certainly pay off as it did for me.

Many nights I would cry, *(some say men don't cry)* well I am in touch with my feelings and that's the best time to write poetry, which worked well for me, as I was able to connect with the raw negative energy and found that so many words flow into my mind (The Abyss).

My struggles with work, life, and death of friends and family really showed me the true value of life and living and the ability to write such great material to inspire others and in doing this it has lifted me up daily and put a smile on my face amidst of whatever is going on. So Today I can stand and give a positive testimony of breaking free from the dark abyss created by negative, depressive thoughts, broken hearted relationships and illness.

I am a true success and will continue to assert myself and assist in contributing to others in their journey to enable them to reach their goals and getting out of their dark Abysses.

IT'S ALL ABOUT ME

A—Adorable, cute and cuddly even

I—Intelligent, charismatic and friendly

N—Noble that's just who I am

S—Sexy, no need to explain for I am the real deal

L—Loveable, just sums it all up

E—Excited, Energetic, Edible even

Y—Yummy, when you think it's the end you are back for more.

MISSING YOU

I am missing you girl
And this I know that you are aware of
I am missing your every touch
Your kisses and that thumping beat of your heart

I miss your body as we embrace
As I look at your face
As it lightens and glistens
Just then as your pussy moistens

I miss the passion and wild fire
That rage you inflict on me time after time
As you climb on top of me
Pussy dripping, pulsing with the rhythms of my heart

Girl they say diamonds are rare
But you are rarer
No one can compare

You are second to none
Body of a Goddess,
Nipples, lips,
Endless fun . . . .

You're everything to me, this I know is true
Whenever you are not a around,
My world turns blue
I need you in my life now and forever more
You are my light at the end of the tunnel and this is for sure

You've tickled my . . . everything
You make every muscle in my body move
Pulsating, gyrating, uncontrollably
My heart beats thump . . . thump . . .
Just for You,
Beats that last and go on forever
Just for everything that you do

MY INSPIRATION

I have searched near and far
For someone to love and care for
Someone who will always be by my side
Always . . . . and forever
Someone who will be my right hand partner
My partner for life
Someone to laugh with,
Someone to play with
Someone to share intimate times and sad times with
Someone whom I can call my own
And call upon whenever I need them
Someone who will always be there for me
And I . . . . for her;

Now today I have finally stopped searching
Why, you may ask?
It's because I have found you
This void is now filled
My heart is no longer empty
For you are that special someone
Who shares!
Those deepest darkest secrets with me
And those intimate thoughts.
Laughter is never a dull thing
For you are my four seasons
My autumn, my winter,
My summer, My Spring
You are my inspiration
You are not my first,
But you are my last,
You're my . . . . everything.

CELEBRATION OF LOVE

You came into my life
And changed me
Spell bounded by your charm
You've made my life complete
For you have cared so much
Being there from the start
Never will I hurt,
For you will always have my heart.
To you I will give my undivided attention
For you honey I'll give everything
For today I make my solemn vows
And together we will celebrate
Our union of love . . . .

For we have come so far
Through trials and tribulations
But together we stood strong
Because of our love,
Our bond,
Our union,
And as I walk down the aisle
To consecrate this such union
We shall place our love into a circle,
And together we will be
In our declaration for each other
In the celebration of LOVE

THINKING ABOUT OUR FRIENDSHIP

Here I am sitting all alone
Thinking of you
The thoughts about how sweet you are
And the things that you do
That makes you a star.
A star in my eyes
A friend, a lover, significant other

From the first time we met
I knew from that start
You had entered my world
And captured my heart
I couldn't resist
So I asked about you
Cause I didn't know . . . .
Know how you would react
If I had came to you
And stated or placed my feelings on the table
So instead now I waited until I was able
To channel my true feelings
Not wanting or waiting
Until you were vulnerable

It's been a long time since I met someone
Someone as nice and sincere as you
Honey I honestly shall
Treasure our friendship now
Yes I do.
Thanks for being a wonderful friend
Thanks for being YOU.

KNOWING LOVE

I would rather know that you don't love me
Than to have to wait for your love;
For one minute you care
Then the next you shove
Shove me around like a putt on a table
Not a care where or what happens
Just as long as you are or think you're able
To satisfy your urge, need, curiosity.

I wish this was love that I feel
Hmmm . . . . But its not
This fucking thing is just so unreal
Unrealistically, just a fucking nightmare
A big joke, maybe that's why you stare,
Stare and laugh at my sorry Ass.

Who would have thought?
Once you really cared
Or so at least I thought
Maybe it was affection I had bought
As I needed love so a partner I sought
But got neglected,
Devalued, hurt and rejected
What happened?
Where did I go wrong?
This love that I thought
This bond which was so strong
Now broken-hearted not a care for me
Just broken promises are all I ever get
This isn't love . . . . this is Bliss
Knowing love can never be like this.

BEING ALONE / LOSING THE BATTLE (LOVE)

Every day and night I sit alone
Constantly I cry as I miss my place called home (Love)
I should be on holiday, enjoying myself
But I am not, as my heart aches
Fighting for freedom,
Now I constantly fight for love
When will this all end?
When will I break from such a trend?

I think with me I hurt because I love too deeply
Is this wrong, my love disperses immensely,
Falsification and rumination of pure bliss and fabrication
Encrusted deep within the turmoil raging within me
Like a volcano, soon I will erupt and all will hate me
For only the gnashing of teeth will be heard
While the rumbling and movements become absurd.

We all strive to live and survive
This has become our main desire
Some live to hurt
While others hurt to live
Why? They know no better
As they play with hearts and emotions
Arranging peoples thoughts and perceptions
Re-enacted day by day, night by night
Some of us can't go on so we give up this lonely fight
The fight to live in love . . . .
The fight to go on . . . .
No . . . No . . . . it's not that we have not lost
Just no need in fighting losing battles anymore
Why waste energy on a fire that's run amuck
We look at our lives and we take stock
Nothing . . . . There is nothing to gain
For our hearts can't go on to take all this PAIN.

THE LOVE LETTER

Hi Boo,

      As I lay here in my bed
Wrapped with Duvet up to my head
Just thinking solely about you
Oh how I wish,
I could have been in your arms at this very moment
As I so long to touch
And feel your embrace
As we sit and talk
And look at each other's face.
Oh how I long
To extend your tongue from your mouth
As it peeps out amongst those
Rosy succulent lips to meet mine

(Sigh) Oh how I long to run my fingers through your hair
Along the nape of your neck
Embracing every curvature of your body
Honey, I look to the day
When I can touch
And bask in the richness
Of your body
While relaxing in your arms
As we gaze at each other
While listening to each other's heart beat.

I so long to touch . . . .
Touch those thighs with my tongue,
And culminate at your Honey jar
Where the honey is always fresh
I so long to delve between your thighs
And taste your Royal jelly my Queen.
I long to sip . . . .
Sip on the sap that oozes from your body.
Honey as I lay on my bed my body aches
As I toss and turn
Picturing you in my mind
Reminiscing of the good times we will share . . . .

Signed your Boo Ainsley.

To the one I adore, I long for you . . . .

BEDAZZLED BY SWEET SEDUCTION

I stood there on my porch, looking out beyond the lawn
The figure I see, voluptuous, dazzling such a beautiful form
I could remember her eyes sparkling like sapphire
Piercing at times like a missile about to fire
I was now mesmerized as I could see the water dripping off her body,
This had left me tense, hmm, frozen mouth drooling.

I remember quite well, when we were young
We would play hide and seek in the back yard or play ground
She wasn't all that, but who would have thought
That once Ugly duckling could have transformed into such a swan.

Her swim was now over frozen still I was
As she drew near to me and to the house
I tried to move, even wanted to hide
But I couldn't.
But as she drew close then said hello, I uttered Hi
Are you going to beckon me in?
Inside my head I said why,
This will cause trouble, but for her I couldn't resist
Temptation was imminent.

I found my voice we chatted and shared a few laughs
Just then I mumbled next time honey, call me to go have a bath
She smiled and chuckled, of course my hon.
I thought it was a frisky one as she rose and showed her cheek bun.
Her legs now unravelled from beneath the wrap
My heart beating, racing, this seems like a trap.

I felt her lips, down, they came close to mine
One little kiss our arms then became entwined
She held me close; I allowed my body for the embrace
As the water from her hair trickled down upon my face;

She pulled apart after our tongues locked for some time
And gently held my hand in hers, looking into my eyes
She softly said this is the beginning, of a wondrous thing
You can be mine and I will be yours
For many years when young we played the part
Now we are all grown you can have my heart.

MY SOLEMN SWEAR—I LOVE YOU

Since I've met you
My world has changed,
In so many ways.
Honey you are perfect for me
Like a ring made to perfection
Created by the finest of Jewellers
And so I've made up my mind
To stay with you . . . . Forever
You mean the world to me
And to me you are my world
You are my . . . . everything
You are my Treasure
Into you I want to pour all my love
All my being

You are my existence, my all
Therefore I give you my heart and soul
I want to be with you always
And as we walk together
Not side by side,
. . . . But as one
And for as long as I shall live
My HEART is yours to treasure
This is my solemn swear . . . . I give.

I LOVE YOU ALWAYS AND FOREVER . . . .

REIGNITING THE FLAME OF LOVE

You have walked into my life and changed me
Rearranged my thoughts, my thinking
I am now more focussed
As my path is seemingly paved,
Paved with your Love
For everyday I shall countless tell thee . . . .
Tell thee how much I love you.

You have moved me in so many ways,
Ways which I never thought . . . could ever be
You have rekindled a flame deep within me
A flame which I always thought was out for good
But now that same flame burns for you
Like the Eternal flame
That spark have ignited the passion and love only for you

Now as I count the days,
The nights seems less apart
Knowing that you are so close within my heart
Its times like these . . . . like this
That I know . . . . True Love exist
And if one only waits
It can be found amongst all the Bliss.

And as each day passes by
I longed to hold you
Touch you, feel your body,
Entwined into mine as one
And plant those sweet kisses that we speak of
Knowing that as this consumes me
Its True Love . . . .
True Love reignited

I LOVE You . . . .

PROTECTION OF LOVE

Petite . . . . Sexy
Down to earth and savvy
Curious smile,
Hidden beneath such beauty
Her lips, perfectly shaped
Oh how I wish I could make,
Simple shapes
Your lips on mine
And mine on yours
Such imaginable things
Should never go amiss
To think of just one, just one kiss
Our lives, our hearts, total bliss
Oblivious to everything around
Nothing matters
But only the sound . . . .
The sound of our hearts
Beating rhythmically as one
Just to think of your touch . . .
Of your hands so soft
As I clutch, and draw you closer
Closer to me
Looking into your eyes
As your body softens
For the first time ever
Now you are in my arms
There you will remain Protected and safe . . . .
Forever . . . . and ever.

WHO AM I?

I am
a part of
you
my love . . . .
I am . . . .
I am the part
that you can't
do without . . .
I am that ORGAN . . .
That organ that sits
more to the left
of your chest.
I am that ORGAN . . .
that beats erratically
when in love . . . .

I sit on your
chest hidden . . .
hidden away from everyone.
out of sight behind your Breast cavity
Where I am protected
protected from
pain,
hurt,
sorrow,
broken,
fail relationships
Please don't let me
get hurt.
Keep me close,
close to your bosom
and I will alert you of danger.
I will keep you in check.
Never will you make mistakes again
For I am you HEART . . . .

REJECTED

Today I opened my eyes
But closed my Heart
So glad at my progress
Glad I didn't start
I would have been traumatised
By the actual outcome
Of her reaction
This caused an imbalance
In my emotions

Now I ponder
What my next move to be
She can be sweet
But so is honey
Too much of one thing
Is not good for me
Now all this has left me with a sour feeling.
Once everything was paved with velvet
Path so smooth a bomb would deflect
But as they say
Everything is just for a time
I presume, there is never a silver lining
How could I have thought?
That she was mine and I was hers
Maybe I was dreaming

But then again I control my dreams
But this was different
This was eating away at me
Like a vulture,
An incurable Cancer
Taking me from the inside out
A total disaster,
My lips always now sealed
Not a word I utter from my mouth

Relationships are hard
Some may take as a joke
But if you don't love someone
Why Stay and choke . . . .
Choke them with your sweet words
Hmmm words which they are not prepare to hear
So perplexed by thoughts
As relationships are lifelong tasks
A task needing great concentration
Just like a painting, a masterpiece
Trying to gain perfection
But instead total rejection
Now no one will want
So my conclusion
Is simple . . . .
Stay Tune . . . .

REALITY CHECK

Can I be the one?
To walk with you in the mountains
Can I be the one?
To hold your hands as we stroll
Can I be the one?
To sit next to you by the river bed
Can I be the one?
To lie next to you as you rest your weary head
Can I be the one?
To massage your feet as you wade in the water
Can I be the one?
To look into your eyes
Can I be the one?
To wipe away your tears
Can I be the one?
To plant those first kiss on your cheeks
Can I be the one?
To kiss your rosy lips
Can I be the one?
If I tell you how I feel
Would you love me?
If I said to wake this is not REAL

DEJECTED AND DEPRESSED

Feeling dejected
Hurt not accepted
What was I actually thinking?
Could this be love?
I really hate this stinking
Feeling
Feeling of disappointment
Where was once love
Is pain and misery
Tightness in my chest
Palms get sweaty
Head starts to pound
I don't like this fucked up feeling
Don't like the breathing,
The sound

I sit with my head in my hands
Crying rivers of tears
Sobbing like a kid
A kid who has had his toys taken away
Only in my case it's my heart
My pride,
My emotions
Everything crashes
Crashes around me
I am aching
My legs go weak
My limbs feel lifeless
Help!
Please help me!

Somebody please help me
I cry out to you
Is anyone there?
Is anyone listening to me?
Just as I feared
No one really cares
Cares about little old me
I might as well set myself free
Free from this world
Where peace and tranquillity would await me
Where I won't suffer no more
Endure no more pain
As I would leave this world
No more light
Only darkness as my lifeless body fades
My heart beat gets fainter
Voices are all I hear
Now I know maybe someone will care
But for whom, or what?
I am gone . . . .
Dejected, Rejected, Depressed, Lifeless

RUMOURS, SLANDER, FALSE PROPAGANDA

People spreading rumours,
Propaganda, false accusations,
Disrupting lives,
That's fucking up the Nation.
To them if they can't get it right
Then it's your bloody fault
You're the main target
It's you that they want.

Unverified accounts
Explanation of events or occurrences
That has no basis
Hurt and defaces
Ones Character
Hurled by un-intellectual beings
Whose only interest, is their gratification
And fulfilling of their emotional state
While lives they disseminate
And re-arrange
Dissolving relationships and breaking bonds.

Why do we let ourselves?
Succumb to such
Immoral injustice
Belted out by jealous
Individuals, sad at everything and everyone
Nothing on their minds . . . .
And I mean absolutely nothing
But to hurt, deceive.
This is how they gain POWER
Or so they falsely believe

We must never bow to silly people
Back biters, back stabbers
Some call them snakes, more like vipers
Ignore the Fools
For as it's written
It takes two to tango
So never let yourself be brought down to their level

For we all know better
So once bitten twice shy
Never let problems get us down
We must always Keep our heads up and stay Strong
Stay Focus and Hold our ground
Cause Sticks and stones
Can only break bones
But words, especially false words,
can do no harm.
So always walk
Head up, Eyes Front
And be Proud of who you are
And what you are about.

A rumour is an unverified account or explanation of events circulating from person to person and pertaining to an object, event, or issue in public concern and lacks a particular definition. Bajan terms—A Lie or propaganda

SAD XMAS, HAPPY XMAS

Ho! Ho! Ho! Ho!
Merry Christmas, Merry Merry Christmas
What's so merry about this day?
When nothing ever seems to go right
Nothing ever happens or comes your way

Tis' the day for us to give love
But to whom shall we give
When all we get is heartaches
Life never is what we expect
Full of misery and neglect

Santa suppose to bring joy and give gifts
But heartaches, no never . . . Why?
It wasn't meant to be like this
For we all need love, companionship
Trust, honesty and faithfulness
So back on my knees
My head in my Hands
I shall pray
Just a few extra words this time I will say
And I hope that this will save my Christmas day.

For even if I am not lucky
I know that I have tried
Not to spread cheer
But to save yuletide
So hope my words won't fall short
And on death ears make me mad
Because I am hoping this will change
And not make my Christmas Sad.

Have a Merry Christmas everyone and a happy New Year. Wish you all the best

WHY—SO MANY QUESTIONS?

How do we measure madness?

How do we measure sanity?

How do we measure love?

How do we measure vanity?

Why is the sky blue?

Why do we have to kill?

Why can't we see the air we breathe?

Why do we have to pay bills?

Who runs the cabinet?

What is it that they want from us?

Why do these figure heads think they can destroy lives?

Why do they have to increase the prices of food stuff?

Why can't they just let us live?

This world is so messed up

God's greatest commodities, taken over, used and abused

Leaving us the general public belittled and amused

At their folly and impeccable disasters and catastrophes

Why? Why?

Unity is what we need

For as United we stand divided we shall fall

Hence together we can then conquer all . . .

For this World is not our Home (Jim Reeves)

For we are all just passing through

But to fit in is very HARD

Fit into what may I ask?

A world of Despair as leaders smile and cheer at our peril . . . .

Why? Why? Why?

So many questions

and little answers.

SOCIAL NETWORKING—FACEBOOKING

I used to wake around five in the morn
After going to bed to sleep around three
This was my typical routine
Since this so-called facebook hype
You might say I am but . . . . hmmm
No . . . I am not addicted
This social networking is just something I like

I used to be big . . . . a big muscular guy
Sixteen Kilos, I was a mean walking machine
Here I am now
A mere shell of myself
Not eating anything no care for food
Who gives a damn . . . Hmmm Fuck Health?
I spend my time exercising my fingers
Speed typing they call it (Mavis Beacon)
Chatting daily, texting, mailing
Applications like mafia wars,
So many games to play
Zuma, Bejewelled blitz . . . . See my high score the other day?

Why should one sleep or even eat?
When we have café world
Where the food is cheap and sweet
No need to worry about food burning.
Or buying appliances is never the same
No need to worry about additional prices
Or V.A.T, cause everything here is tax free
Relationships, hmmm is another thing
Can send love messages, notes and hearts
To any part of the world to your love or your fling
So many choices are there for you
Whether woman or man, boy or girl,

Don't need to leave home to shop
Could plant vegetables on barn buddy or Farmville
And sit back; watch your stock or crop

I don't have to waste my money on postage stamps
When a birthday comes around,
Greeting cards are there for free
I can send one, maybe two, even three!
Update my status later
Let the thieves and crooks know where I am
Giving them ease of information
Making it easy to find me when I am not around
Can also have aquatic life on aquarium or Fishville
Then brighten up my house later on Yoville
No need to pay council tax . . . . why? No, not at all

Could even own or buy people on friends for sale.
How about . . . Are you Interested?
Grab your buddies later
Start your gang on mafia wars
Where the bullets can't touch me,
But step outside in the real world.
Better watch your back or they will get you.
So see? The facebook thing isn't all that bad?
It's full of education, loads of communication,
Otherwise known as . . . . gossip
I don't need to go partying
For you all do bring the issues to me
Posting your photos for the world to see
So in this Virtual world I am KING
So to hell with you all
I will remain socialising!

HEART BROKEN, CHEATED ON

I sit in my Darkness . . . .
A darkness which you have created . . .
Created a monster within me
Full of rage I cry out
But no one hears me . . . . heard my cry
My call is deadened by muffles only I could understand
As I sob and yet wonder why
You have left me . . . now taken another

In your head you created the scene of a crime
A crime which you said I have committed
Now upset and with hatred
Which fills your very soul of me
As I sit and shiver,
Wondering and thinking
Pondering
Why can't people ever understand . . . . ?

Understand me . . . .
Fuck this world now,
For I have suffered way too long
In love, in love now, hurting for a love,
A love that does not deserve;
For I loved from the start
I have given you my soul, all my love, my Heart
Through and through
I have been there for you . . .
I've helped in good times and sad times
But lo and behold,
To my dismay
All I have ever gotten from you was cold hearted HATRED
My heart now filled and overflowing
Beats fading, Blackened, Darkened,
With so much pain
Pain . . . . charred remnants are now all that remains.

To hurt is to be hurt, to love is to be loved . . . .

BAD MORNINGS AND ALARM CLOCKS

Hey boo can I come lay with you
I need to rest my weary head
Just for a minute or two
Maybe on your succulent inviting bosom
My head I can lay
Just looking up at your beautiful smile
Into those mesmerizing eyes I can gaze
As I take your hand
And entwined them into mine
While I lick your bosom sniffing your
Reb'l Fleur off your extended nipples
A scent so sexual
Arouses you, making your juices drip

My hands travel
My fingers glide
And as I touch your clit
You tremble . . . sending waves up your body
Your nipples become so erect
You lick your fingers
Which now turns me on?

As my cock bursts through my fruit of the loom
Like inspection day
At full attention, it salutes you . . . . Darling
I flop on the bed as you grab it by the head
Short strokes, you've done this before
My body freezes, tenses, relaxes
As the shock waves of intimate pleasure and passion
Submerges my entire body

Just then my alarm clock goes off
It's bloody five in the morning
Time for me to rise
My head now pounding
As my Blood pressure slowly comes down
I rolled off the bed to pick the pieces of metal from the ground
The poor cuckoo clock was thrown across and smashed to bits
How dare you wake me at a time like this?
Instant disappointment
To what started so good
Maybe next time I should
Dream a little earlier . . . .

FINDING ME . . . .

Today I cried a million tears
But not one even moistened my now dulled cheeks
Why . . . because my heart would not allow them to be displayed for you to see
But instead the hurt, the pain I felt deep within, became rage
It began to overwhelm me, surging inside
I began to spew angered tones which erupted like fiery lava

I never once wanted it to be like this
But I need to rid of this, this unfamiliar feeling
I gave but never asked of you
I loved but never asked for your love in return

-but in retrospect, I was happy
Happy with how you made me feel
You somehow made me feel good about being me
You made me smile on my darkest day
I was happy

But as the silver moon casts shadows
signalling the end of this day
I know there is an end to this
So as I turn to walk away

I walk away knowing
I am capable of loving unconditionally
I am capable of giving relentlessly, and
I can still be ME!!
So today I cried, but
tomorrow I will rejoice
for I have found me!!!!

Written by Kim N. Nurse

Kim N Nurse is the mother of a beautiful daughter ZJ and being a child of the earth has had a knack for writing many years ago but never acting upon this gift until now. I never called my writing, poetry; I thought of it as an outlet for me to vent and to express my unadulterated feelings, so much easier than knocking out someone or destroying things. Writing took me to a place where unwinding was made easy and to do so without fear of rejection.

My motto in life is be the change you want to see in the world, es ist was es ist!!!

JUST WANT TO BE A FRIEND
NO NEED TO ACT ILL

Excuse me miss
Can I have this dance?
Why hell No! I don't know you.
You are in a club it's just a dance
I am not asking for Romance
Why the need to act ill
Just wanted to be friendly
Isn't this how it all starts

I remember on facebook
I sent you a request.
You reported me
For wanting to add you as a friend
What the fuck was that about?
Only needed someone to play a game with
I was only asking you to be my neighbour
As we play the same

Why behave like you made yourself
All I sent was a friend add
Not a fuck request
I can get that anywhere
You think you are the gift to men

Does this mean you are open for anyone?
That's not what I need.
It's a social network
Where we build and meet people

Why the need to get all worked up
In such a virtual world
How friendship does begin?
Isn't this how it all starts
But you had to give the . . . .
I don't know you
Who the hell is he?
What does he wants with me?
It's people like you that make the world a crazy place
Then on your photos you lock
Cause of the things you got up too
But everybody knows you
No need to hide
Your business on facebook
Has gone platinum, even world wide
So the next time someone adds you
Just think about it all
Before you start to judge.

ALWAYS REMAIN POSITIVE

If someone tries to ridicule you
Ignore
Why would you allow yourself?
To be brought down by such negativity.
Always keep your head up high
And think positive
For the Road to success
Is not to allow
Negativity to get the better of you;
Having Fear is the by product of losing
So Ignore.
Instead . . . . be strong, Erase all negativity
Embrace the positivity
Remain Focus
And you will achieve your goals.

PLAYING WITH WORDS

So much deception
Compounding my perception
Yet I get caught at the Intersection
With love, in love
No fear of rejection
Into the mirror
I saw my reflection
It was very real
Not a projection . . . .

DAILY MISSION—GIVING THANKS

As I awoke from my slumber
I looked to the sky
And prayed to the heavens
To God on High
Thanking him for yet another day
So all my respect I surely will pay.
For I am one of his children
And I am glad to be alive,
Knowing in this world it's hard to strive

I arose from my bed
And set out to start my day
Brushed my teeth, got dressed
then was on my way.
Hopped into my car
Just then I said another prayer
Knowing how people can drive
Along the highways and byways
We should always give thanks
If we so desire to survive.

Cause living in this world
Full of reckless people
Can make living such a big task
Not losing one's life
We must make our time last.
So every minute, every hour, every second
We should give thanks and praise
As we embark on our mission
Each and every day . . . .

THE PRAYER

As I bow to my knees
To the Lord I pray
Please come into my life
And guide me today.
So many things trouble me
But to you I can say
For I know you will listen
Attentively and show me the way
For in spirituality and guidance
Maybe this is just what I need.
As I feel you descend
From the heavens above
Touching me my Lord
Sharing expressing your LOVE
With Gratitude I outstretch my hands to you
Accepting your presence
Which shows as a glow upon my face
Knowing now I can walk high
With dignity and not disgrace . . . .

Amen

FOR WHAT IS?

For what is LOVE
    If you really don't care
For what is LOVE
    If you can't be sincere
For what is LOVE
    If you find it hard not to and to do
For what is LOVE
    If you can't say the words "I LOVE YOU".

MY DREAM

I went to sleep
I had a dream
And in my dream
Subconsciously
I had some thoughts
My thoughts became ideas
This eventually became my vision
    My vision is to be a poet
    A poet with words
    To chill the soul
    Feed your hunger
    Take control
    Control of your mind
Nourishing you with ideas
Splashing colours and new designs
Taking poetry to higher heights
My Dream . . . . Now a Reality

LET'S BE UNITED

History, they tried to eradicate
So much malice, so much hate
Instead of educating us
But they can't
For our great fore fathers and great grand-parents
And further down the chain
Have sweat and toiled
Day in and day out, through the night
To pave the way for us to be free . . . . UNITED

Pain, hurt, malice, these words just cant express
Death, fight for freedom
Many days and nights with clenched fists
For in this world we were seen as nothing . . . .
Bare emptiness
But together we pulled strong
Giving a good fight for the cause
Blood tears and sweat
Are now all we can recall
So now to this day the fight goes on
On a much different level

Whenever I look around
It hurts and brings tears to my eyes
To see through all the encounters and struggles
Brothers and sisters still killing daily
At the amusement of others
There are just something's we haven't learnt
And likewise some will never change

Still hurting and paining, hustling and bustling
When will we ever be free?
How can we be able to stand strong and tall
Well . . . . With spoken word / poetry we can do this all
Educate everyone
Just open up your hearts
Let's stop the fussing and the fighting
For only in strength and in numbers
We can stand together . . . . Make this happen.
Conquer all
And be UNITED

FORGIVE US FOR THE MESS

Once we were like broken pieces,
Shattered beyond reality,
But we held together as pieces,
Strong,
We broke free of all the negativity.
Tossed about like feathers in the wind,
Never knew where we would land,
Some passed, looked . . . . not wanting to lend a hand.
Looked down upon us
In our tattered form
Deformed in their minds
As we begged, borrowed and steal.

Steal so that we may live
But live, for what life?
A life of drugs and crime
Hoping we won't get caught
And possibly do time.

We were having fun,
Or so it seemed
But time to wake,
Wake from this fucking dream
A dream . . . . which we would never like to relive
Our minds and brains tattered
Full of holes like a sieve

Our hearts were hardened
We never knew love
Yet sometimes we would pray to Him above
Looking back now it hurts deep inside
For we have damaged . . .
Way too many lives;
How can we pay for the damage we have caused?
When we were pieces, broken . . . . Shattered . . . . without love.
Stop, never, play, rewind, pause

Given one chance too many
Now we reclaim our lives
The journey that took us to the bottom of the sea
Was now over
It was our last ride
Rock bottom they call it
No more places to hide.
For we were once a shell of mere reality
Looking out . . . .
Looking out beyond the fragmented pieces
Now given the chance
Our lives can now be mended . . . .

HOW CAN WE BREAK THESE SHACKLES?

We were held back . . . . back in time
Reality became an endless void
That fight proved futile
So many nights we wept and cried
Pain and hurt
Scarred minds, bodies and souls
Friends and loved ones taken away

Oppressed with memories
Is all that remains
Within in our minds
That we stand today to break free
Break free of those shackles
That once bound us
In captivity, enslaving us
Creating diversity among each and everyone

We were once tools
Tools of the master trade
We were used and abused
Broken . . . broken spirited
Bashed, lashed and even killed
Killed at the whims of the then Masters

None of us want to be captive
For to be a slave is truly mentally challenging
But in this world, some choose to make a switch
Switching their man made shackles for religious ones
Thinking everything will be okay
But how can this be
We have become a part
A detrimental part of history
History . . . how can this be erased

To this day it still remains
On a much lesser scale
But we shall continue this fight
For it's our right to be free
Freedom of mind, freedom of speech
Liberated for what we stand for
We must all come together and be one
One united family
With one common goal
This goal is . . . .
FREEDOM

VIOLENCE CAN NEVER BE JUSTIFIED

I awoke this morning had a real banging headache
Words in my mind, such racial hate
What can I do today should I kill a coloured?
Who the **'Fuck'** can I aggravate?
I couldn't settle, my mind was racing
Everything seemed so chaotic
I called a 'homie' let's go shoot someone up
All these violent thoughts
Such rage, just racing through my mind
How can this ever be?
These thoughts can never be defined.

I am such a good kid always on the straight and narrow
How can this be, how can my life now be marred
By all this rage inside me
Willing to take the life of another
I am only a man, mere mortal not a mother
I can't give life, so hence why should I think about taking one
That's somebody's daughter, nephew, niece or son
It all doesn't make sense to commit a crime
Doesn't make sense
To do all this killing
How can one justify
When they took part and was willing
No need to beg for mercy
You were there from the start
You were the one wielding the knife
That went straight through the Heart

Now I look at the news in the Old Bailey
No mercy shown for **Stephen Lawrence**
Yet you sit calm, No remorse, no time to contemplate
A boy who did nothing wrong

Yet you both carried so much hate
You took his future,
You took his life, his family and friends
Who made you God?
There was a beginning you put the end
The end to a life . . . .
A life that can never be restored
Now 18 yrs later victory must be shown

It took a seven week trial
Thanks to new technologies
DNA Testing
So now we've got you by your testes
For such a heinous offence
Which should have never come about?
But you all held malice and hatred in your heart
Because of the colour of one's skin
Now in prison hope that you are scared and have to hold your farts
And watch your backs everyday
Cause one way or another
You will more than likely have to pay . . . . dearly

Justice is served . . . . is it?
But did it fit such a crime
One . . . . Fifteen years, two months
The other . . . . fourteen years, three months
Is this truly justified for a life?
What about Damilola Taylor?
Also Trayvon Martin,
They suffered such the same fate
When will all this violence cease?
Why do we have to carry so much HATE?

Why should the colour of one's skin justify if he or she should die?

WHAT MY COUNTRY MEANS TO ME?

Barbados is my Country
Of which I am extremely proud of
So no matter wherever I go
I must always show my love.

For my country as small as it can be
My dedication to my flag remains
With its colours blue, yellow and black
Symbol of a broken trident
Showing its separation from the Union Jack

A country full of life and vigour
Splashed with entertainment of calypso music
Bands like Square one, Krosfyah
Exotic places to see, beaches and liquor

Not forgetting the nightlife and scenic beauty
Lots of places to shop, for your every wish
Later spend your time on the coast (Oistins)
Enjoying your favourite dish of coucou and flying fish

My Country I am a true Patriot of
For none other can compare
For this is my country **Barbados**
Which I love and will always show I care.

WHAT IS LIFE?

What really is this life that we speak of?
For we are not here that long
Some taken away from old age
Some taken away from young
For we are born into this world
And we learn to love and hate
For we are taught to survive
So friends we seek to make.

Throughout the changes in life
And all the struggles that we go through
Whether good or bad
We have great people around us
Called friends,
And no matter what,
They will stand together by you
As they make us who we are
and contributes to everything that we do.

But why do we have to be riddled,
With so much pain
The pain of Life
The pain of Hurt
The pain of suffering
The pain of Death
For we are here but only for a short period
So what really is Life?

I AM ALWAYS WITH YOU (CRY NO MORE)

Why do you stand and cry?
Why do you weep?
Are they tears of joy?
Please wipe the tears from your eyes
And cry no more
For I am not gone
I will always be here
My presence,
My Love will always be felt
For this is our connection we share

I will always be with you
So please cry no more
I am merely resting my head
As I was tired,
Felt Weary
But now I am happy, as I needed this
So here I am
No more pain, No sorrow
But I must say sorry,
Until we meet again my friend
Another day, another Tomorrow

You may feel sadden
Please don't worry
But I ask of you one thing
Smile daily for me
As I will always walk by your side
Hand in hand
But in another role
As your guardian angel I'll be.

There are no goodbyes for us, wherever you are,
you will always be in our hearts.

THE BLACK WIDOW

She was every mans dream
Hot, sexy and beautiful as ever
But her mind was wasted
As all she ever thought about
Was to hurt and fool everyone . . . .
Everyone she came into contact with,
She was like a black widow spider,
Deadly and conniving, deceitful as can be
Spinning her web, thick far and wide
Eluding no one as they all get stuck,
Stuck Inside of her grips,
Venom so strong,
Web . . . . Long strands, stretch far and wide,
Spun' . . . .
Purposely just to trap.

Her glance frightening as she trickles her body along,
Ass upright, cock back, outstretch so long,
She feels you tug on her web,
Just then she pounces out to wrap you in her arms
Hugging closely but this is not a love embrace
It's the spin of death
As you feel your body goes numb . . . . lifeless
As the air becomes thinned
Your lungs collapses, she has won
You are no match for her

After she abuses and uses
Feeding on your very life
Getting everything she wants from you
You are discarded like a piece of wrinkled cloth
Tattered left to be chew on by moths
Stained, no more uses
Lifeless, Drained full of bruises.
You are partially dead
No longer part of this chain
Its natural instinct
Survival of the fittest
You are her provider
She is . . . . The Black Widow Spider.

Beautiful yet Deadly

GLAMOROUS UNTIL DEATH

There she goes, beautiful as can be
Sexy figure, well poised, big booty
The way she walks and whines
Shaking her ass . . . . damm she looks fine
She is the hottest thing around since the lava flow
Got everyone talking, making her face aglow.

She is like the next top model
All the guys drool and crave for her
Maybe she can be compared to oxygen
As they cant seem to get enough
But whatever it is they eyes just pop
And just a glimpse makes they blood pressure drop

Strutting her stuff,
Elegant and Glamorous
She flashes a smile
But beneath she hurts and cries
For all we see is her outer shell
Like a shiny stone
And this is not who she really is
But through years of hurt and pain
This is all she knew
And how she would cope

Dressing the outer shell (a mere facade)
To hide and encompass
Her grieved and traumatised ridden soul.
She continues her journey
Within her heart all the joy and pain untold

She comes to the end
The End of her journey
Still all alone
Glamorous, Beautiful beyond imagination
But without a soul
It's her last ride they say
Ashes to ashes, dust to dust
For this is true reality
This is a must
We can't hide from Death
When our time is up
This means there is no more left
Nothing to bother about
From Dust to Dust
Back to hence we came.
The moral of my poem
Never worry or think that you are alone
Let others in to hear your cry
Then things will never be the same.

TRIBUTE TO MY BUDDY— AHMED APPLEWHAITE

Ahmed you were the only one I could talk to
Share my deepest secrets and my laughter
Now all this is gone shattered lost just like that
As you were taken away, now my life is a disaster

I knew you were in pain
And I knew how you felt
Cause many a days we would talk
And it all would make my heart melt
Just seeing you there sick,
And nothing I could do
Made me felt bad inside
And I knew you knew
But I tried to keep my composure
And our routines never changed
Cause we would still hang as we used to
Now that's all a mere memory
But those I would hold onto.

You were my friend
Actually still is
And forever you will always be
So where ever you are
Just remember me
For I . . . . will always remember you.
Sincerely, forever your friend
. . . . Ainsley.

Written on 08.06.11 @ 01:22am
Copyrighted by Ainsley Carter—Author n Poet of Poetry a way of Life

TRIBUTE TO DAD

In Loving memory of our Dad Edmund Bradshaw

Dad we miss you so
It's a true shame and sadness
That you had to go
Just remember you haven't failed us
You have done well
And we will shout your name out loud
A Daughter (Shurla), son (Ainsley)
We will make you proud

For your name will be heard
For many a mile
As we sing yearly rejoicing
A true friend, a hero you were
Never neglecting
Always helping and forgiving
We remember just like yesterday
For now only, are memories we have
For you were a friend, and a wonderful Dad
Memories go, memories will fade
But Dad we will remember you each and every day
For in our hearts, that's where you lay.

Our dad our Hero MAY YOU REST IN PEACE

IT WAS A VERY SAD DAY . . .

There was a silence,
You could have heard a pin drop
As the news broke,
She couldn't grasp anything
As it all came like a shock
Teary eyed, she tried to wipe
Wipe away the pain, the hurt
She grabbed his hand, as he lay sedated
A lover, a friend, husband
All she had in this world

The news then spread
I received mine by text
When it came I felt my heart jumped
My head started to pound
I was exercising, I could do no more
To my bed I went
Only to wake a few hours later
Shaking, shivering, remembering, my buddy, my friend
We have been through so much.

Eating away at me, I fumbled
And struggled to pull myself together
Just then I got another text
Reading with trembling hands

I wondered, what's next
It said, had his surgery but, continues to bleed
Hope these surgeons succeed

I prayed at that very moment
For God to pull him through
For friends and loved ones
We are here for you,
My pal, my friend, my Buddy Ahmed
For you were always there
Now here I am . . . . but you are not here
But my Friend,
My comrade we will always care.

My Friend Ahmed was sadly taken away from us on the 26th May 2011,
Gone but not forgotten. God had a better plan for you buddy for now you
no longer suffer. We will all miss you.

WHAT COLOURS REPRESENT TO ME?

Let's talk about colours
What do they represent?
White for instance
Symbolises purity, divinity, to be angelic
Brown, reminds me of the earth
Where we came from, our Birth
Yellow, a picturesque to behold
Bright as the sun, some call it gold
Wisdom, joy, intellectual energy
Green, reminds me of the grass
Earths precious layer, nature or fertility
Blue, skylight, as natural as the sea
A picture of youthfulness, peace and spirituality
Red means to stop, a sign of danger
A sight most of us never likes to see
Action confidence, courage and vitality
Orange, this is nature's secrets
Of vitality with endurance
As she calmly paints the sky
Illuminating the evening, the sunset we see
Black, a colour to be proud of
Some associate with evil,
Symbolises death, or stability
As it dominates everything else
Then there is grey, Ashen as the skin colour
Symbolises sorrow, maturity and security
So all the colours together
Influences how we live
Our emotions, our actions
Just a few of things
A part of our everyday life
Our Bio, Psycho, Social, Being.

RISE OF THE BERRIES

I have tried everyone
Now it's time to reveal the test
There's simply none other
So forget the rest
I tried Apple, Nokia, Sony and Motorola
And none can surpass
As the Black Berry is the Best

With smooth details
Keeping everyone on their toes
Cutting fast technologies
Power of the BB grows
For the young and old
Far and wide
In the city and villages
Everyone knows BB
No-one can hide

To link all you need is the BB pin
And you are on your way
Messaging, sending pics
Cultures they are all the same,

It's a BBM world,
every household should have
So it's a must
Grab the latest models
If it slides it's a plus
cutting first class
Innovativeness
Pure craftsmanship, slender designs
sits perfectly in your hand
while your mind races
As you become engrossed in every detail
Menus changes,
As the wallpaper dances
Across the screen
just then . . . . A PING is heard
And your BB lights up
a message is in . . . . You smile
as your fingers caresses every button
Climaxing with send
now relax as u grab tighter and tighter
As BBM addiction becomes your enlightener

TRIP TO THE DOC

I took a trip to the Doc
As the pain got worse
All I wanted was for it to stop
I kept popping pills
And nagging everyday
Just wanted comfort
Just wanted it to go away

I got there and so many people were waiting
I said it couldn't be they have the same ache as me
So many noises filled that little old room
Just then my name was called
And I was hustling to get a pee

These docs nowadays
They want blood, faeces and urine
Crazy isn't it,
What is it that they do?

Are they selling it?
Doctors are crazy but hey . . .
What's up with my voices?
Doc I need a cure
Am I schizophrenic, bipolar maybe?
Please doc would you help me,
When I speak to God you say that I am praying,
But when he speaks to me
You want to section me under the Mental Health Act 83"
Maybe nothing is wrong with me?
Maybe the whole of society is crazy
That's what I think
Maybe they all need help,
But what can I do?
This world is sick doc,
This assessment is through
You can't help me,
I am here to help you

THE ECLIPSE

As the night settles in
Darkness covers the land
They all scamper in doors
Babies, children, woman and man
It seems like the end of the world
But that's far from nigh
As everywhere is pitch Black
As it engulfs all the light (bad taking over evil)

People are screaming not knowing
What this phenomenon is . . . .
It's merely an Eclipse
This happens about one in every six months
But way back in the days
Man was ignorant to this fact
Thought the world was over
As everything went from light to pitch black

Now in this era
It's all crystal clear
With star gazers and scientist proven test
We now get to understand their theories
That the end of the World
Is far from near;
So next time this happens we give thanks to God
For in his eyes we must onward Plod

NIGHT CRAWLER

As the sun sets across the lands
We stealthily crept out of our bonds
Shakes ourselves, while smelling the air
The time has come; this was our time of day

As we group together to plan our haul
To reach back on time before dawn falls
Upon us unleashing, it's fury of fire
For this is something, none of us desire

Some have the ability to travel by air, others travel by land
Searching the streets, as fresh food is at hand
Through the alleyways we crept
Our first victim, we pounce straight to the neck
For this is the way we feed
Drawing blood fulfilling our craves
Hoping and wishing, drawing back quickly
Trying not to make them as our slaves (humans)

It's not a nice thing but what can we do
This is our survival, our livelihood
For we have but two greatest fear.
Not forgetting sunlight, another hindrance
The slayers with their crosses and stakes of wood
For our movements are shunted by these
Through our hearts they woods may pierced
For Vampire Slayers they are killing to please

UNITED AGAINST DRUGS

Women
Sex
Crimes and thugs
Stealing,
Killing,
Mugging
All because of a life of drugs
Crack,
Cocaine,
LSD, PCP
Marijuana,
Pills and Alcohol Killing Society
Taking the young, getting rid of the Old
There is no discrimination
The Drug Takers and Traffickers
Killing us out
Putting our Nations on Hold . . .
Families are no longer . . . .
For they are broken apart . . . . ripped at the seams
Fancy clothes and cars
Are all just temporarily . . . .

Some people become murderers,
Some stick to petty crimes
Prostitution more prevalent
Stop a minute . . . .
Its everyday life
But Alas! Hold up . . . . all is not nigh
Please understand
We don't need DRUGS to get high
Turn the "Telly" kids to BBC 1-5
Education starts here should we want to survive

It's a life of Crime
A life of shame
We should really stop to Ponder
It's not really a game
For we are taking lives
Killing one another
Our Uncles, Aunts, Mothers, fathers
Our sisters and brothers
Our family . . . . As close as we are,
Yet we seem to destroy.
When we stray so far
We forget about the church
We party more and more
But Alas there is a solution . . . . Please it's not a cure
Let's all UNITE, BE TOGETHER
And stop this problem getting to our door
For to solve this Catastrophic Reaction, we must fight
To conquer the WAR on DRUGS,
We must UNITE . . . .

United we stand a chance to win any battle. Let's form organisation WAD.

W—War
A—Against
D—Drugs

STRENGTH DESPITE TRIBULATIONS

I am like the tree
  As I sway in the wind
    Watch my limbs rock
      And my leaves rustle
        I shall not be moved
For my base is securely anchored
  And my roots spread far and beyond
    But why do you try to rock me?
      Why do you come to rustle my presence?
        How have I angered thee?
Alas I trouble no one . . . .
  You with your Axe and saw
    Powerful you are
      But my bark is strong
My ROOTS spread far and wide planted firmly.
        Yet you cut me down
    But I shall only spring forth again
      For I too am strong
        I have withstand Hurricanes, storms, floods
          But man my worst enemy
Why do you hate me?
I give to you shade when you need
I shelter you by allowing you to use me and my family
For lumber, building your houses, cottages
        Yet still you return no gratitude . . . .

GET UP AND STAND UP

You soared high above the sky
Looking down upon everything and everyone
Scorning, preying upon the weak and helpless
But we were more in numbers than you ever expected
Yet still you took us one by one
Waiting till we were vulnerable
Crying out for help
Going astray . . . .
Then you seized your moment
The opportunity . . . .
You had us in your grasped
As we were taken away
To be eaten / made as slaves

But little did you know
That way down deep within our clan / tribe
A strong one would emerge
With nothing else but Victory on their minds
Not to be preyed upon ever again
A leader for the weak and vulnerable
To take us out of this,
What seemed like a bottomless pit;
To fight, for ourselves
Fight for Freedom,
For what is right

No one deserves to be bullied
Ridiculed or spat upon
That's why we need to rise up
And be as one
Unity and Strength equals Freedom
For as one we may not be seen
But in numbers we can make a STAND.

Don't be bullied by anyone, stand up, speak out, seek help, make your dreams a reality, Reach high, be like a flower blossoming and blooming to be heard. Your voice is your tool. A simple Pen can be your gateway to freedom . . . . Write your thoughts and put them into action. For the pen is mightier than the sword.

THE JOURNEY

want to kiss my way from
toes to fingertips
making the trip
s   l   o   w   l   y
taking in all the sights along the way
noticing the little scar on your knee
from the day you fell out of the breadfruit tree
and tracing the rough edges of the place
where mosquito bit—leaving a trace
of her love bite
and I do the same,
soothing with a kiss.

silky thigh makes me sigh with
softness of tender skin
wandering,
my tongue has thoughts of plundering . . .

I pull it back into line
and continue my journey
tracing each curving hip
with heated breath from questing lip
I pass over the rolling hills of your behind
remembering the first time
I saw your birthmark

I have no haste while
arms encircle willing waist
not wanting to miss anything,
I stop to take in the view
how breath taking!

You
are exquisite, so divine
I start again the meandering climb

carefully scaling sloping spine
with kisses.
Tongue plays connect the dots
drawing lines between each freckle
but not to draw a picture
I'm seeking all your pleasure spots
Gently parting flowing locks
I make my mark on nape of neck,
teeth carving, "I love you," into tender bark

Kissing slowly down shoulder blade
noting carefully the Goosebumps made
as trailing fingers trace your back
lips close to journey's end
I suck each finger—turn over
now
for the trip back
d
o
w
n
.

.

to your downy
mound . . . .

Written and copy righted by Robert Gibson aka PassionPoet

Robert R. Gibson is a poet and spoken word artiste that writes out of a heart of sensuality and passion; so much so, his stage name when he is performing is Passion Poet. He enjoys painting sensual images with his words and leading his audience into a sensory experience. Although sexuality and sensuality are his main forte, in his own words he says, "Passion is not always about sex." Passion is anger, sorrow, enthusiasm—all powerful emotions including seduction and sensuality. Thus, his poems are written to evoke powerful emotions. He has been writing from age 14 and is aiming to have his first anthology of poems published soon.

You can check out his blog Poet: Whispers at http://poetwhispers.wordpress.com.

THE LUCKY PEEPING TOM

There she stood
Long slender legs
So smooth
Tempting to touch
Her contours
Beautifully crafted
She was my coco cola
Shaped woman
Tantalising
Hot tamale
Finger licking like KFC
She meant everything to me . . . .

Yet all I had was misery
Every day I would rush home in time
Just when I knew she would be there
In from work looking fine
Stripping off her uniform
She goes into her shower
I could feel every water droplet
That touches and covers her body
I could feel her breathing . . . .
She bends, cocks her leg up on side of shower
I go on full zoom
Bringing her closer to me,
I so wish I could touch.
Her mound protrudes between her legs
Her lips,
Visible,
So pink
The Dove soap that she uses glides across her body
So effortlessly

What am I doing?
Is this wrong?
Am I invading her space?
I know she sees me,
As she peeps up and smile
She has to know this has been months
Such a long while . . . .
She grabs the razor from the ledge
With gentle strokes,
Her once hairy legs
Now glistening;
So silky smooth;
She steps out of the bath
Stands in front of the window as she creams her skin
My heart beats as she backs me . . .
What if she turns?
What would she think of me?

I saw her later that day
At the corner pub
She sat with the shortest skirt ever
Her legs spread apart as if inviting
Now I was so shy
Should I?

Could I?
I walked over
Words we exchanged
Her voice was so soft
But my promontory was erect
And all on my mind was her in the bath.
She sprung the question on me
Why do you peep?
When you can simply come over and knock on 69
I couldn't speak just in my perverted mind all there was
Was that number . . . . that position . . . . Room 69?
Licking those soft silky smooth legs
She was as bold as she was stunningly beautiful . . .
Her hands found their way on my thighs
She knew what she wanted and I obliged.
She unbuttons my pants and grabbed it in her hands
And said "I am not wearing any panties"
That's when it happen
I shot my load all across her hands
And onto her face . . .
Embarrassed I was but she was gentle and caring
She smiled and said
Let's go back to my place and get cleaned up . . . .

Stay tune for part 2

REACHING THAT CLIMAX

I want to hug you, squeeze you, and grind you
Kiss on your cheek,
Girl I will never leave you
My legs you make weak
Weaken by the way you handle me
Showing so much love
Abiding by the rules set out by Confucius
Guided by the thoughts of Solomon
Just then I kiss your lips
Burying my tongue into your bosom
Through the valley between your rows of mountains
Sending you now into oblivion as my tongue
Slowly embraces your nipples like a young . . . . Sucking its mothers bosom
Your body now shivers as if you're shocked by electricity

This sends pulses through me
Telling me that you need me
Needing more and more
By now your top flies off across the room
You wrapped your legs around me
Lifting your body up to mine
Your fingers sunken deep into my back
Just then my shirt you yanked off
As my lips now travels around your navel
Gliding on your body

I inhale the sweet aroma of your Belgian chocolate body
Just as your legs divide allowing me to feel the heat
emanating from your Honey Jar
Your juices runs making me slide all the way down
Your hands ruffles my hair and pushes me lower
As my lips connects with the pointed tip of the heart cut shape of your pussy
You arch your body sending the tip of my tongue touching your clit

As you moan you wrap your powerful legs around my torso heels into my back
I clasped my hands on your hips
As I anchored my tongue around your sensitive labia's

Gently I pull on the outer lips
Then licking the ever flowing juices from your canyon of sweetness
Your erectile clit stares at me beckoning me to suck on it
I form small circles and lick up and down imitating a Snake
As my tongue covers it all
Just then my lips forms a cover,
As I suck on your hard clit
Your nails now dig deeper into me
Just as I slide my protruding tongue into your now gushing pussy
You explode projecting your juices into my mouth

Your body is heated now as you pull me up
I placed my promontory cock at the edge of your lips
And with small circular movements I tease your mound
Then I slowly plant it deep inside as you moan as every inch slides in
As it touches inside your body which is now so heated
I begin with slow thrusts and as my momentum gets faster
You bite into me as we have a cool rhythm
You can't hold it in and climax not once but twice again
You mumble for me to cum the third time with you
As I spun you over entering you from behind
Grasping you hair you arch your back
And as I am about to cum
You push your body right back on me,
For everything I got which I now plant deep within you
And we both explode together
Reaching an exonerating climax
Flopping down onto the bed
I feel my once promontory cock going limp
As we cuddle and caress our juices drip and runs free
Bringing the perfect closure to a wonderful evening . . . .
An evening to remember . . .

HOT! HOT! PASSION

She was as fresh as the summer breeze
Her skin as soft as silk
Her lips so soft and subtle
Her breast, two round moulds
Oozing sex appeal, dripping at my touch with milk
Her body calls to my every touch
My hands glide along the contours
Her body arches and aches for more
She has never been touched like this before
As my lips soothe her aching soul
Circulating her abdomen, her navel
As her legs then buckle and divide
As if calling me, beckoning me to enter
Enter into the gates of her heaven
Her place of solace smells of freshly cut roses

My lips travel along the inner thighs
As her back arches, she lets out a moan
Clasping my head with her hands
She groans, louder and louder
Her hips now swaying from side to side
Pushing her upper torso
While pulling me closer
My lips now touch her outer labia
She digs her nails, deep into my back in ecstasy
Calling out my name
As I gently pull apart her outer lips
Then the inner ones
Exposing her now so sensitive clitoris

Her juices, flow continuously
Like a river, flooding the embankment
She tasted just like my favourite
Caramel and coconut
My tongue searches, as I push deep inside
Her rhythm becomes more intense.
My body now rises to the pleasure
As I licked her now warm protruding clitoris,
She moans and groans
So intense, as her body responds
Begging me to go deeper

Her body is hungry with emotions,
An intense deep sexual urge
Ready to taste the ecstasy of my tongue
Blood rushing, pumping through both our organs
She screams, I'm coming please don't stop,
Louder and louder, sounds like thunder rolling
My tongue now moving like a jack hammer
Up, down and side to side
As she lets out a rip roaring scream
And pulls me deeper into her
I can't breathe now but who cares
As she climaxes, bringing the first part to an end . . . .
Bodies tense then relaxes as I caught my breath
She looks at me with sheer pleasure
A deep sigh of satisfaction fills her body
Her pussy still pulsating with waves of ecstasy
Her hunger satisfied until next time . . . .

HOT! HOT! PASSION (PART 2)

She gently brushed her hands against mine
I reached to touch her, holding her hands in mine
She led me across the room
To somewhere more private
We sat and talked about old times
I could see from the mischievous glint in her eye
That she wanted me
I could read her mind, and as she touched me
I felt the heat radiating from her voluptuous body
Just exactly what she wanted,
What she was all about
Just then her fingers touched my mouth
She leaned into me
And planted that kiss
The kiss of life
Her lips made the most perfect shape
Covering my mouth
Her tongue now deep into the back of my throat
Her hands finding their way under my shirt,
Her fingers gliding across my chest
Caressing my body, hmm
Her hands so silky soft, smooth
She kisses and nibbles my neck
All this time working her hands down
Along my abdomen to unbutton my pants.

Her lips now caresses my navel
Gliding along my body
She gently slides my pants off
to take a peak beneath.
My now promontory cock stood upright
As her hands circles over
Yanking it out

Like a greedy person, but full of passion
Clasping her lips over the shaft
Her body moves up and down
Sending shivers throughout my entire body
There is a need to scream
A scream of ecstasy as her body gyrates
Gently swaying and bobbing
I looked at her
Beckoning her don't ever stop
Just right there I told her
As my now protruding manhood
Became so pronounce
With head swollen, veins pumping with blood
Filling her mouth
As she lets out a gasp
A calm sigh
As my body now stiffens with so much delight
Every muscle tenses, hormones raging
She took me deep back into her throat
My gosh, I screamed, legs went weak
I wanted to say "fucking hell" but just couldn't speak.

Her hands gently caressing my nipples
My body now tormented, so much emotion
My head felt as if it will implode
Just then my body erupted violently
Sending all my love juices squirting
Into the back of her throat
Composed and calm she continues her mission
So intense it was as she looked at me and smiled
Hope it was worth the long while
I was lost for words
Limbs became so weak
HELL Yeah! I mumbled . . .
But just couldn't speak . . . .

I KNOW WHO I AM

Educated, Tough, Mature I am
People oriented, never to be blinded
For you my audience
I will be your lyricist
Listen to my words
That spews forth from my mouth
Poetry in motion,
For this is my new Love.

Putting my thoughts together
Words I form
Sentences, paragraphs
Acronyms, synonyms even Bajan Dialect
Are just a few forms coming from your local Poet!

Listen closely because you are the ones
To grade me on my style
While I punctuate my lines
Creating my vibes
Transforming, meta-forming
Into a unique being
Different styles, same charm
Culminating my art

Since the year 2000, that's when I started
Now here I am ten years down the line
I punched myself
Is it really me?
Eluding all negativity
Only Positive—that's who I am
Bringing cheer to the Nation
Even on the rough seas I make Calm

I am not professing to be the greatest
But I am Unique
Creating styles
Evidence in my rhymes
Not patronising
Nor belittling
For that's not my cause or belief
For in my Heart
I am for everyone.

I am a Stalwart, a soldier
Together we are, but an army of one
United, forming standards
Conforming for one DESTINY . . .

SUCCESS

I am the pinnacle
This means I am at the top
Staying here is hard
But this is where I intend to stop
I am a true success
With GOD by my side
I know I am truly blessed
Working my way up
Was a hard struggle
This included dedication
And true commitment
Long pain staking hours
This paid off for the cause

To be Successful in life
One must face all tribulations
As if being put to the test
And go head on with full determination.
To achieve one's goal
Might seem like a fairytale
Things will be unbalanced
As if on a scale
Yet one has to be bold
And persevere to get there

So Life will not be easy
As some may want you to believe
Some will try to deter you
Get you to go astray and leave
But standing Firm
I held my ground
Planted solid
And now I am still around
. . . . To tell the tale of my success.

BE CAREFUL HOW YOU DO IT

Into her mouth it went
as it beat and bash
against the side of her cheeks
sometimes feeling as if to choke.
She took it up and down
in and out
soft,
sometimes hard strokes
being careful
yet not wanting
to lose her momentum
her mouth full of it
the whiteness
should she spit
as its advised,
or swallow
which is not an option for her

As it's advised that toothpaste can cause Harm . . .

THE TEST

She placed me into her mouth
I didn't think it would fit
The length, the width
Thought it was too much for her

She had clearly done this before
As she pulled back the outer skin
And gently placed it into her mouth
Savouring the taste as she moaned

It was near orgasmic, 'she said',
I have never had one this good
She was now glad to be a Tester
For the new
Chocolate!

CLEANLINESS IS GODLINESS

There she was
Standing there
Ushering
Tempting
Teasing me
To come lay with her

I quickly obliged
Stepping out of my clothes
I gently got on top of her
Writhing slowly
Smelling her
Stroking
Rolling
She was cold at first
But then quickly became warm
As my body heat spread

She had just changed her attire
The smell,
The feel of Egyptian cotton
Was par to none,
Against my body
Felt so heavenly
Nothing feels better
Than to be lying in a new bed
Covered With fresh linen . . . .

SENSUAL PLAYING

Lips locked
Sensually
Bodies heated
Momentarily
Clothes thrown all over
Cuddles
Slurps
Exchanging of saliva
Juices dripping
Constantly, flowing
Passion, pain
Screams of ecstasy

Slapping
Pounding
Bodies in motion
Caressing
Stroking
Thrusting
Lots of yelling

I'm Cumming
'Give it to me big boy'
Showmanship of strength
As they slammed
Smacked . . . . Onto kitchen counter
Coucou stick
As a paddle
Whips and crashes
Over buttocks, reddened
Marks etched,
Bruised
All in Love and fair play . . . .

BAKING

She just stood there
Looking at me
Paled
She needed heat to be completed
Are you ready yet?
I tasted her one more time

Then I stuck it in
Just as she became engulfed with heat
She began to rise from the bottom
And spread wide over
More heat needed
As the cherry oozed out the middle
The cake was now finished
Browned at the top
Remove from oven.

GROWING UP

She was born into this world
A darling she was
Such a beautiful form
Smiling ever so sweetly
She was given to her mother
And in her arms she laid
Close to the bosom
For months here onward she will stay
Sucking
Clinging in the bondage stage
Happy as a lark
No hatred, no rage.

As days went by
This new world she would see
To explore with feelings, touch, love, curiosity
Now as a young toddler grown
Great values, parents will bestow
As she learns more and more each day
Questioning,
Seeking answers along the way.

Life was now,
No longer a mystery
But a challenge to her
Trying to find, what is right from wrong
She explores her new territory.
Now a teenager she is grown

Changes in anatomy, was not expected
Explanation given by mum
Taken in not rejected
Guidelines, rules all re-enforced
For her to take heed, not to ignore

Now a young woman
The true test begins
To try out all that she learnt
Building relationships
Pain
Commitment
And try not to get hurt
But these are all keys in growing up
And can never be avoided
These are life's lessons
To make mistakes
And learn from them

Middle age and married now
Just as mum had taught
Her own kids and family
Lessons, learnt has paid off
She's one out of many
Who got to fulfil their dreams!
That road from life to death
Remains a struggle-
Mystery . . . .

REVENGE

Skirt flew
Thrown onto back
Penetration inevitable
Crime committed

Sick to the stomach
When will this end?
Would someone please HELP!

Ridiculed, life taken away
Now depressed
Wrecked from the inside
Scars in memory
For years to come

Traumatic events
Continues to unfold

Tormented she screams at night
Afraid of the dark
Remembering that time,
Constantly
As she was ravished by a monster

Bruised, destroyed
Emotionally
Physically

Perpetrator walks
Now time has been served
Allowed to roam
Five years after
That's all he got
Where is the justice?
Now her life has been distraught.

Afraid, ashamed
Protection needed
She brandishes a weapon
A 9mm to be exact

He doesn't forget
Tries to jump her once again
Gunshots
Way from a mile can be heard
Only this time
JUSTICE IS SERVED.

GETTING INTO HER

I stood there watching HER,
trying for the longest time
to find out why?
Why was I drawn to HER?
How could I?

She looked,
ever so sexy,
smooth,
And I knew with just one touch
I could turn her on
I knew the power I had in my hands.

But for a moment
I thought to myself,
When I do turn her on
Would I ever get into HER?
I then realised that it would be much better,
For myself and everyone else
If I just leave her alone.

I don't ever think I could,
have paid all that cash for HER
Just to watch HER
That new SONY BRAVIA 42" 3D smart TV . . . .

MY SUNSHINE

You are the sunshine
In my life
You have brought me happiness
And Joy
An everyday I look forward
To BB'ing you.

Your voice notes
They make me smile
The calmness and sweetness
In your voice,
Relaxes me,
As you laugh,
This send chills through me
Yet I am afraid
Afraid to say how I truly feel
For fear that you may not
. . . . may not be thinking the same
And as we know rejection hurts.

But on second thought,
Seeing that you have expressed
How you look forward
To hearing from me

Makes me feel joyful
Knowing that the love I feel
Is reciprocal
And special
And only to think
That now we are on the same wave length.

I admire your smile
The pictures you send
Captivating, depicting your sensual body
Exposing your dimples
Captured by your cam
All this just for me
I do take note
Of every detail about you
And for that
I am glad you stepped into my life
Knowing it's so easy to chat to you now
As we have so much in common
My Love
    My friend
        My sunshine . . . .

LOVE HONOUR AND RESPECT

A woman is a woman
But what really differentiates them
Is it their hair styles?
Maybe her figure
Is it the way she sway her hips?
So full of life and vigour.
Is it her boobs?
Or maybe the size of her booty
What really is the message?
that we are conveying
What is it that we are saying?
God made man in his image,
Beauty comes from within
The outer appearance
will always fade away
Like yesterday
was
and is no longer
today.

If you are to love a woman
Love her as you find her
Be respectful
And always be kind to her
Don't call her names
Don't try to change her.
When you met her,
She was a seamstress
Yet you wanted her to be your mistress
Now you say she is no good
As she couldn't live up to your demands
Your expectations
Was she not what you first wanted?
Back then you should have left her
Or stated your needs in the beginning
Not waiting until it develops
Then you go change your mind
That you can do with ideas
But not another person's feelings
Women should be treated
Like princesses and queens
Not cast aside
Or treated like second hand property
Or like someone's rejects
Treat them with love honour and respect.

COLLECTION OF SHORT STORIES

IT WAS A COLD NIGHT AT WORK

Written by Ainsley Carter

It was a cold "winter" night and a few stars were out in the sky. I remember this as if it was just yesterday.

I was alone at work on the night shift working as a security guard at "Ace's Law Firm". I had just gone into work for 20:00hrs and took over from my friend Brian. Brian was a tall big burly guy from the Caribbean Island of Trinidad, and a very cool friend as well. Sometimes we used to go partying on weekends. Brian told me just before he left that Sandra would be back to collect something she had left in her office and would be back from her banquet as soon as possible as she needed to also get some paper work done for the next day.

I had just sat down by the front desk, when to my surprised I saw her car pulled up into the parking lot. It was a red Ferrari slick in colour and nature, All I could think about is driving in that car. My eyes now focused on what was about to happen. The car door opened and out popped one of her legs so beautiful on the night screen and my heart started to race, only if she noticed me. Hmm she won't want anything to do with a poor old security guard at all. So many thoughts crossed my mind. Just then out popped her other leg, wow a pair of the most gorgeous, sexy glistening legs I had ever seen, and they belonged to this amazing lady who had me mesmerised and captivated by her beauty, entrapped deep within my mind.

She stood up from the car, pulled her blue skirt down and tidied herself and bent over to take something from the car. She had the most perfect booty I had ever seen, so round and her skirt now stuck onto her hips with a small split up the back showing a small portion of her panties. This was too much for one brother to take and I surely didn't want this recording for my colleagues to be watching. This was just for me and me alone to see. Just then she stood up, closed the door and headed towards the building. I now tried to tidy myself and look busy. She walked over to the door. That walk was so sexy. She was a head turner and had been divorced now two years. Her husband also had worked in the building and was one of the big bosses there. I remembered him as he had had a fling with one of her friends in one of the offices and this was caught on camera which he knew nothing of. Poor guy as he was as nice as ever. We used to train in the same gym for over a year but I never knew she worked here and I never imagined he had such a beautiful wife, why would he want to hurt this lady. All I could think about is how perfect, so symmetrical her body was.

She came over to the desk to where I sat, by now my legs were trembling. She said, "Good evening, I haven't seen you before." I am just going to my office to finish off some paper work, it shouldn't take me long. I buzzed her in and was admiring her from behind, just then she turned and smiled at me, as she entered the lift. As the door closed I thought to myself it's the perfect opportunity for me to make my rounds.

I secured the door and dimmed the lights to the entrance of the building making it hard for anyone to see in through the tinted glass panels. I was just so excited to see her at work. On making my rounds when I came to the 10th floor I heard a sobbing and gently opened the door which was ajar.

There she sat head in hands next to the photocopier, crying her heart out. I cleared my throat and said, "What's the matter". She replied, "That she was just going through a tough time and this was the reason why she had come back into work. I stood there and we talked and being a polite gentleman I asked her if she would like a cup of coffee. We walked over to the Lunch room where I made her a cup of Kenco extra strong while she sat on the sofa. I strolled over handing her the mug and my hands touched her fingers which were so soft. And as I was standing I could peer down into her bosom. She wore no bra and I could see her pert nipples. At this time she quickly held her head up and caught my eyes fixed to her chest.

She smiled and asked, "Do you like what you see?" I hesitated for a moment but shyly said, "Yes", in a rather low tone.

She asked me to sit and drew closer to me; all this time inside I was smiling, thinking this is the best job in the world. Here in front of me was the most gorgeous woman with skin so soft.

At this point I had completely blocked out my thoughts about my woman, Shelly, at home. It wasn't hard to block Shelly out of my head as all she ever did was nag all the time and accuse me of doing things unimaginable. Shelly was from Barbados but came over to the USA five years ago with the intention of becoming a mode. She ran into problems fighting and was badly beaten. That was the end of her modelling career as her body bore all the evidence of her battle. Her dream ended before it started.

Sandra slipped her hands in mine; they felt so warm and then buried her head in my chest. By then, I reached my arms out to comfort her. While in this close embraced she brought her head up and all I could smell was the sweet scent of Anna Swarovski perfume. That scent was so appealing and although she had just returned from a function it was as fresh a scent as if she had only moments applied it. I could feel the heat emanating through her clothes as her temperature rose. She brought her head up and our lips touched. That's when all inhibitions were now through the door.

We kissed passionately. Her lips so soft smelt of strawberry lip gloss or lipstick. Her tongue elongated, found its way into my mouth lashing the sides of my jaw so intense and full of emotion. She ripped my blazer off and my shirt next and threw them across the floor. Her top, I was trying to slowly to remove but to no avail. I was crap at this. Her skirt had by now ridden way up to her waist.

Our lips came apart as she unbuttoned my pants and I stood up and stepped out of them, she then pushed me back onto the sofa and climbed onto me, her legs pressing against me. I decided to take charge and with her legs wrapped around me lifted her up onto the table. Sandra leant back arching her body and brought her knees up onto my shoulder, as my tongue caressed her now fully erect nipples. All the time I was thinking of how silky soft her skin felt. I could just picture this happening on many more occasions. My tongue slid down her bosom and from her movements I knew she was as hungry as I was excited as she pushed my head down to her pussy, now dripping wet with her juices. From her moans I could tell she never had it done like this before. He legs clasped tightly around my neck now as I licked her clit and her warm pussy juice slithering down my throat.

She was fucking amazing, as I clasp my hands on those hips and buried my mouth. All I was thinking now was that I had better perform at my best, couldn't let this lady think I couldn't handle a beautiful curvaceous lady like her.

I was at it eating her for a good half an hour while she climax over and over again and she could squirt. By now I had slipped out of my boxer and she grasped my cock in her hands and as we reversed positions. She was at it like a pro as she began gently massaging the head of my cock with her lips in small circular motions which had me on the edge of the table and so many times I was at the brink of shooting my load off but managed to hold myself back somehow. There was no way I was going to cum and not have this cock in between those warm legs pressing against that mound.

She gave it all she had and she was now ready to fuck. Bent over the table, I entered her from behind. It was uncomfortable at first for her but she wanted my big cock. I worked it slowly inside of her and she was gently pushing back for it. It was now firmly inside and I was giving her soft slow strokes, but she stated she needed it and wanted it hard and rough, so I obliged. She sat on the edge of table and spread those legs apart and I pounded that pussy as she screamed out in ecstasy. As she was about to cum I slid out and she shot her cum onto my chest. I quickly entered her once more and pounded that pussy, grabbing hold of her hips, as she dug her nails into me. I lifted her and we stood pressed against the wall, only if walls could talk.

By now I had her bouncing on top of me as I held her firmly. She stuck her tongue deep into my mouth, as the beads of sweat trickled down our faces. This was what she was missing, been a long time coming. In my head I was so glad for making that switch to cover that night.

I gently rested her on the sofa and placed one of her legs on my shoulder while I stuffed that pussy from the side. It was now red and she took her hands and massaged that clit while my cock slid in and out of her. I was beginning to feel my love juices building up and pounded her harder as she grabbed that sofa for dear life. By now half her buttocks was off the edge and just as I was about to cum she felt it and slid off me and grabbed my cock with both her hands and clasped her lips around my now bulging, throbbing cock summoning me to shoot my load into her mouth. She took it all in and opened to show me that she had actually downed it all. I flopped on the sofa as she climbed onto me and we held each other in a tight warm embrace, cuddling and kissing. She said, "Thanks", that was the best fuck she has had in many years. We sat there talking for a while stroking each other's body and it seemed like we had known each other for a long time.

We made fresh coffee and sat on the sofa chatting . . . since then, this has been our nightly rendezvous.

THE FANTASY VACATION

Have you ever had a fantasy? Well my fantasy growing up was always to be with a woman. I loved how my hands felt on my body and always wish another woman was making love to me, until that weekend when it all became a reality.

It was August 25th some other girls and I had taken a trip to Grenada as it was one of our friends Sasha's birthday. We had landed in Grenada at the Maurice Bishop's Airport. It was a beautiful place not huge but pretty and the people were friendly. We were all a bit tipsy from the flight, as we drank loads of spirits back on the plane.

I remember about 30 minutes before landing, my friend Carol who sat next to me close to the rear of the plane was so drunk and kept leaning onto me resting her head on my shoulder, and occasionally stroking my legs. We were used to playing around so I didn't think much of it, until she tried to kiss me and as her lips came onto mine I pulled away and we chuckled.

Surprisingly we got through customs very quickly and hurried outside to the taxis. They were six of us and two of the girls were a little padded around the hips so we had to squeeze into the taxi. It was fun and at the same time a bit crowded but luckily we were all friends. Fortunately or unfortunately enough at the time I sat on carol's legs and that ride was long hot ride as it was summer time and we were in one of the tropical islands. The roads were long and winding but the sights were exquisite.

Halfway through the journey I could tell Carol was getting a little frisky and I was thinking maybe it's the drinks we had. Her hands evidently found its way under my blouse from the back and she gently played with my spine rubbing gently and at this time I allowed it but looked at her in a shocked way and she just smiled at me.

Carol and I had been to the same secondary school and lived close to each other. She was a very reserved quiet girl so this had me quite shocked. Funny enough it felt really good to know that another girl fancied me and in my head my fantasy was playing over and over like a stuck record. At one time I even rested my head on her shoulder and none of the other girls said a word. I was now wondering if they knew what type of person Carol was and what would they say to me.

We suddenly arrive at our destination a beautiful Hotel with a large swimming pool. The Hotel staffs were very courteous and polite. We were shown our rooms which were two double rooms with three beds in each with an adjoining door so we were practically still together.

It was about 22:00 hrs when we had unpacked our stuff and I took the bed by the window and Jane jumped in to share that bed with me. Jane was a slender girl, 26yrs of age and never yet had a boyfriend. She hardly had boobs on her chest and got teased quite a lot. I remember when we were in school the guys thought she was one of them and she played along, joining in their sports. Carol shared a bed with Susan, who was a 27 year old brunette, adored men but never kept a guy longer than a week. She had such a reputation, so this trip was going to be absolutely fun for her, as it was right up her alley.

Susan wanted to go out on the town and hit the night clubs and so we all got dolled up and headed out. We arrived at a club called September's Night Club, and it was nice. The decor was somewhat of a summer theme blended with ancient Egyptian statues and Water fountains, dimmed with red and blue lighting. When we got to the dance floor the music of 'Krosfyah', 'Pump me up', was playing so we all started to party as we loved the Calypso music. Carol grab hold of me and was whining on me and gyrating while the others were teasing her on.

She felt really good as she clasped her hands on my hips and we swayed from left to right. The night felt perfect. The other girls bought some bottles of wine and we all just drank and kind of let our hair down.

I began to feel sick and darted to the toilet followed by Carol who went to use the toilet while I puke all over the sink. She came and washed her hands and asked, "If I was okay". I washed my mouth out and turned only to have her plant a kiss on me, which took me by surprise, and as drunk and sick as I was I obliged and we kissed and laughed. It was at that time then she said, she wanted to do that for such a long time, but had never gotten the courage. I responded, That I wasn't that way inclined but it felt good. My body was reacting to her in such a way that scared me, and in my head I wanted it to never stop. She had awaken and aroused such sexual feelings in me, and just as she was about to run her hand up my legs, we heard the outer door to the bathroom open and quickly separated and giggled while pretending to peer into the mirror.

We were now back on the dance floor and partied for a few more hours before heading back out to our hotel.

Back in our room the girls were so tired they all just plopped down on the beds and fell fast asleep. Carol and I had other plans and cherished that moment. She was gentle with me as it was my first time. We walked into the living room on the big red leather sofa and she kissed me again, and as her lips touched me my body trembled wanting more. We took each other clothes off and lay on the sofa. She took her hands and placed them in mine while she kissed me, my body now felt as if it was on fire, my nipples were erect and tingling and I quickly spread my legs over the back of the sofa while she came directly in between them.

She was just kissing me and sending all these sensations through my body. Her lips paid special attention to me, sucking on my neck, my nipples which by now were so aroused and sensitive and as she touched them I arch my back rising slowly off the sofa.

The room was dimly lit as the light from the street lamp outside shone through directly behind the sofa and I could see a sparkle in her eyes that she was satisfied as she got what she wanted, while in my head I was thinking the same. My last boyfriend never caused this fire to rage within me at all.

Her lips travel along my body to my navel as she pulled gently on my skin while her hands caressed my nipples at the same time. Her skin and touch was so soft and gentle. She knew exactly what she was doing. As her lips touched my waist line I bit my lip and using small circular movements with her tongue she came around my vaginal lips and my hands grab hold of her shoulder. The tip of her tongue barely touched my now erectile and overly sensitive clitoris and I let out a loud moan. Carol was a Sagittarius which meant she was a strong lover who enjoys strenuous intercourse and will make love throughout the night, while I on the other hand was an Aquarian who was curious and uninhibited and would make love whenever—and wherever—the urge strikes. My favourite position was usually standing and bending over for a sexy quickie but in this case that was ruled out.

Carol's tongue flickered around my clit and it felt crazy and was driving me wild. The sensation felt like she was licking an ice-cream and all this time I could feel the pulsing of my pussy and as the juices flowed she slurped it up. That noise alone drove me crazy. She clasped her hands under my buttocks and lifted me gently with my assistance as she sank her tongue into my pussy making up, down and across movements. I couldn't take this anymore and wanted to pleasure her as well so I told her to lie on the sofa which she did and this gave me time for my pussy to cool from the intense simulation.

I quickly went about between her legs as she was already so aroused and the smell of Chanel lingered around her vagina, my favourite fragranced and this made me go wild as I nibbled on her labia as she grinding her hips as if she was dancing on my face. The hair on her vagina was neatly shaped into three circles interlocking which I thought was so cute. She also had her name tattooed just above the waist line in Algerian lettering.

Carol was somewhat very kinky indeed and I was willing to find out how much. I stuck my tongue in her and tasted her love juices which were so damn sweet and was just flowing like a river. I could hear by now our neighbours were awaken and heading out. The sun was peeping up a bit and shone down upon us across Carol's breast. I was eating her like crazy and just as she was about to cum she inched back and got up and we both went into position 69 as she said she wanted us to come together. I preferred to be lying on the sofa while Carol was on top and we ate each other. At times the intense feelings got so much I just let out a few sighs and in no time we both had cum and Carol the expert she was squirted her cum all over me as we both then cuddled up together.

We both had forgotten where we were and nearly got caught in the morning when the girls got up but it was a night to remember for me. My fantasy finally came true and with one of my best friends.

THE HANDY MAN

It was coming onto the hurricane season, and we were way behind our schedule because of the lack of funds. Because of my wife's Jodie's surgery things were becoming increasingly hard as I had to do lots of odd jobs to make ends meet and also care for her. It was really sad to watch her lying there at times. She was paralysed from waist down due to an accident involving a drunken driver who had no license. My wife's car was badly smashed in the head on collision and this was her result.

The Driver, Steve McLaren was an ex police officer and had left the force 5 years ago for aggravated assault on a minor and being intoxicated. His licensed should have been taken away but the criminal system always sucks like this.

I would work at the Candy's Hardware Supply and ever so often I would deliver and fixed anything for the customers.

It was a Sunday evening while at work I saw this beautiful lady strolling into the hardware store, and came over to me for some advice and assistance. Her name was Alana and she had the sexiest figure ever and a lovely nice ass, which filled her blue Levi Jeans to its bursting seams. She wore a slinky green short top and was showing her perfectly shaped abdomen, and her pierced navel. She was an absolute stunner. Around her neck she wore a beaded chain with a little stone but this was not the only piece of jewellery as I looked and noticed that she was wearing a wedding band.

She asked about the prices of bathroom and patio tiles as she wanted to do some remodelling and also where she could find a good dedicated worker to do the job for her. I thought about the idea of the job and said that here at Candy Hardware we usually deliver at a time convenient for her and that I could take a look at the job she wanted and be of assistance.

She chose a beautiful bluish colour with a floral border for the bathroom and some new Terracotta tiles for her patio. These were the new stock which had recently arrived from Hawaii. I made my plans to come over the following day which was a Saturday after I had finished work. I then followed her to the car and she gave me a business card with her details and she quickly got into her silver Mercedes Mclaren 2010 model. It looked so slick and as she sped off out of the car park two of my colleagues came over wanting to know what she wanted and who she was. One of the guys Jonah said to be careful of her as she looked like trouble but hey, what did he know, he has never been with a girl, poor guy.

I finished up my work and was all smiles that evening and as I got home I was met at the door by my wife's carer who was in tears. She broke down in my arms and told me that my wife had just passed away. I was in shock and dropped on the staircase in awe. I knew this day would come but not at a time like this. I was shattered and couldn't speak and the other family members were arriving as we all gathered in the bedroom until the coroner arrived. She laid there looking so peaceful and out of pain. Inside I felt relieved for her as it was unbearable to think one minute you are walking around then the next all your dreams shattered. I buried my head in my hands and asked, God, "Why"? That night I didn't want to sleep alone at all and then I thought about my job the next day, so I called up Alana and told her what had happened and asked if I could make it another day instead, to which she agreed and gave me her sympathy.

Two weeks had passed and the funeral was here, I was in a much better frame of mind now as my family and friends were around to give support. We arrived at the church which was packed with so many friends and family, Jodie was well known as she worked as a hair dresser and that's where all the ladies would flock and chat.

The Priest gave a great sermon and after the burial we had the wake at a nearby Guest House, which I found out later was close to Alana's house. I was shocked to see her at the funeral but didn't get a chance to say hello. That night at the wake, I got really wasted and just passed out and missed everything and everyone.

It was exactly one month since I had met Alana, and I decided to call her up, and to my amazement she was waiting on me, which brought a smile on my face. I needed to get away and to do the job to get some money to repay a few debts and finish off my project. We had made arrangements that Friday and I drove over to her place for 4pm. I pulled up into her driveway and it seemed so long from the house. I was met by an electronic gate, some huge palm trees and some people working trimming her lawn and watering the flowers, it was a beautiful place and the house was magnificent, with a water fountain in the middle close to the front of the house in the roundabout. It was the perfect dream house.

I wondered what made her come out to get the stuff in the first place when she could have easily gotten contractors to do the job.

I was met by two ladies who worked for Alana who ushered me into the house and sat me down, but said, 'that Alana wasn't in as yet but will be with me shortly'. I had barely started to sip my wine that was brought for me when she stepped through the door, wearing a multi-coloured wrap revealing the heart shaped front of her and matching bra. Not to be missed with the cutest tattoo of an eagle on her chest.

She greeted me and was very polite, enquiring, how I was feeling now after my loss, and how I was coping. We chatted awhile and she said she had met my wife briefly from having her hair done at 'Top Flick n Chic' hair salon. Time flew by quickly while we chatted on various topics and before you knew it her workers were bringing us supper. This was beyond my expectation and after all this time, we still had not spoken about my purpose for being there. I was still wondering how such a gorgeous lady lived in such a huge house and had no husband or boyfriend or close friend. Later that was explained to me, that her husband was a rally car driver and died and since then she never had been close to anyone but rather kept to herself' as she knew how men would flock to her just knowing what fortune she had.

After supper we kicked back on the patio drinking Malibu and pineapple. I enquired about the work which she showed me and it was a tremendous job. I gave her an estimate including materials and the price but she wasn't bothered at all. She wrote me a cheque for $15,000.00 which she said had nothing to do with the job. I was shocked and didn't ask what it was for.

We continued to chat for a little while long and then I bade her good evening. On arriving home my family members who had stayed on after the funeral were curious about the meeting and I showed them the cheque. That night I got a call, from Alana who thanked me again for coming over and wanted to invite me out to a banquet the following day. I quickly accepted the invitation.

I was a complete stranger at the Banquet but she kept to my side throughout introducing me as her close friend. This made feel important and very 'big headed'. The meal was lovely, it was done with a Brazilian theme and endless food and wines were served. I felt like a king with my queen at my side, but in the back of my mind I was thinking of Jodie and what she would be thinking. This solemn moment showed on my face and she quickly gave me a peck on the jaw and I responded with a smile.

Music by the late Whitney Houston was now on and she took me to the dance floor, where we partied until we were both tired. The DJ quickly took the tempo down to a soft ballad and we locked arms and swayed at the back of the room, by now our heads were spinning with the alcohol.

We left in her chauffeured Limo and went back to her house. En-route there we kissed and as her lips met mine she looked deeply into my eyes as if saying, 'welcome to my world', and in my mind I was asking myself, 'Is this heaven'.

The driver pulled into her courtyard and opened the doors for us as we staggered into the meeting room and then into her living room. This was not how I wanted a moment to be like if it was to happen but we were not in any state for anything as we both crashed out on her sofa, only to be awakening a few hrs later by soothing music playing through her sound system which was set to come on at 10:00am. I was startled and she awoke in my arms and thanked me for the night. She had to be at a meeting shortly and I had to rush home as well.

All this time I kept thinking about her, so beautiful she was and her skin was so soft which responded to my every touch as we danced that night.

The next evening I went over to start my work. The temperature was about 35.0 Celsius and so I took my shirt off as I worked showing my ripped hard abdomen as I listening to my music. A few hours had passed and as I was digging the tiles up, I never saw her approaching. She had been watching me from across the room admiring my physique. She greeted me with a smile and said she loved what she saw. I was about to ask a question and she came over to me and planted a wet kiss on me which took me by surprise, I quickly dropped what was in my hand and lifted her up and took her to the settee on that Patio, she was wanting me and I needed her. We were like two hungry animals. I haven't made love to another woman since my wife's accident so I was going to pour all my emotions in her.

Her kisses were so passionate and soft as she wrapped her legs around my torso, I took my vest off and ripped her blouse away exposing her bra which was off in a flash and staring at me were two beautiful headlights and the beam was her nipples which were so erect. I buried my head between her rows of mountains and licked her breast, tasting her perfume, she smelt so dam good and as my tongue travelled down to her navel I picked her up from the sofa with her legs wrapped around me as her hands unbuttoned my pants which I quickly stepped out of. I placed her firmly onto the sofa which was huge and shaped in an 'L'. She put her head firmly onto the arm rest of the sofa. I slid my way down parting her legs but she wanted to tease me as she quickly closed them. I forced my way gently as she resisted but still assisted and as my lips touch her labia's her hand grabbed my hair and she said, "I haven't had this done to me in over four years", I was very gentle and licked the left and then the right labia, then passed my tongue down the centre of her vagina tasting her juices, so sweet it was and as I lapped it up she was working that waist. I grabbed her huge hips and cupped her bum into my hands and brought her up a bit. I then placed my tongue on her now erect clit which was pierced, then putting it between the loop of the ring giving it a small tug which made her moaned. Her fingers were now buried deep into my back, and as I stuck my tongue deep inside her pussy she dug deeper into me. Her vagina felt so warm and smelt really good, her juices were now gushing at me and I was circulating that clit with my tongue in snake like fashion. I could tell when she was about to come as all the muscles tensed and then she shot her cum at me splashing my face.

She now wanted me badly and I lay back while she came between my legs and quickly grabbed hold of my cock in her hands and with a tug it was in her hungry mouth. She had me on fire and as I was about to cum on several occasions she stopped me by squeezing around the head of my shaft and then tickled the tip sending me over and over again into the heavens.

She was now ready for me but I pulled her up and she sat on my face, her ass spread all over me and I stuck my tongue once again into her and she came once again.

I placed her to lay on the sofa on her side and I tease her pussy with my cock just placing it at the entrance to her pussy then pulling back then she quickly grab me and slowly guided me into her. It just went in like it was made for her. Her walls were throbbing and as I went deeper she was moaning and groaning. It was about just 4" inside her and I wanted to sink it all in and as I did she screamed not in pain but the pleasure she felt. I was pounding after that as she called out my name, all this time I was hoping that none of her workers were around. She was noisy and I gave her my all until she came over and over.

We changed positions and she got on top of me and rode my cock until I shot my load into her and she flop onto my chest and snuggled up in my arms.

We got up after 5 minutes and went to her bathroom to have a shower together and having sex in the shower was the bomb as I placed her leg on the wall and rammed that pussy from behind as the water beat down on our skin, it felt good. She was satisfied and I was fulfilled. Since that encounter we have been living together and having the greatest sex ever. She is an amazing woman . . . .

THE TEMP

It all began one Monday morning, I remember quite well because I had just returned to work from my annual leave to beautiful Barbados. That was the most exotic holiday I ever had, so many places to see on that remarkable island. The most enjoyable thing was the unbelievable hot and spicy fish with salad served in Oistins.

I remember sitting in my office that morning, when I heard that accent and looked up to saw the most beautiful sight one could behold. Her hair was worn in long black locks which bounced as she modelled her stuff. Her Dress was not the boring black everyday sight to behold but the beautiful Caribbean colours I had seen on my holiday. She wore a nice V-neck blouse which sat symmetrical with her chest only displaying a small percentage of her cleavage. I looked on in awe as she approached my office for her interview.

I could see from the others reaction that they too were stunned by the gracefulness of such a beautiful creature.

Immediately I called her in and we introduced ourselves. Her name was Ingrid and she had been living in USA for a while and was now living here in London for the past year. My first take on that was why leave USA to live in UK.

Ingrid had been a secretary for a number of years and that was perfect for me, as I wanted to know nothing else, she got the job. I took her around the office and introduced her to all my colleagues and showed her where she would be working. What caught my eye was the way she looked at my friend and workmate Jo. Jo was a sexy blonde lady, in her late 20's, who was not only attractive, but remarkable in bed. She knew how to please any man, and her wide knowledge of kinky games was a plus.

I remember when I first met Ingrid and we hit it off in the photocopier room. That was the most explosive quickie I ever had. The photocopier room was way down the hall away from everyone. I had sent her to do some printing for me and I forgot one of the papers which I needed so I took a stroll there. Now Jo was a lady who knew what she wanted and would just go for it, so as soon as I got there and opened the door, it was like she knew I would be coming and grabbed me by my tie and closed the door. Her hands felt my now stiff cock bulging in my cotton slacks.

She planted that kiss on me and my hands automatically touch her panties which were now soaked with her love juices. Just then she bent over the copier, yanking her skirt up onto her back only to reveal her blue thong which I pulled to one side. With hands reaching back she took my cock out guided me into her clean shaven pussy. I completely lost all my senses. There was no thought of being caught.

I began with small strokes and her moaning was turning me on more. I pounded her from behind as the adrenaline rushed through me, from doing such a daring act like this.

We were at it like 'jack rabbits' until we came together and I shot my spunk all inside of her. That was the best five minutes ever and the start to our afternoon secret sex romps. Many times after that we would find new places to have our daytime quickies. It became a regular adrenaline rush.

Later that day I receive a text from Jo which said, "That she loved Ingrid's look and she would love to try her out". I replied, "It sounds good to me just fill me in so I could watch".

A few days had passed before Jo stated that during the week she had dropped hints, flirted with Ingrid in a joking way and that the response gave some promise.

It was on that Friday two weeks after Ingrid joined the staff that we were the last ones to leave the office. Jo had somehow managed to get Ingrid in to assist her and with expectation and anticipation received a ping on my Blackberry to come in five minutes.

I finalised what I was doing in haste and took a quick walk down the corridor to Jo's office where the door was left ajar, in anticipation of my arrival. I could hear lips smacking and on peering in I saw Ingrid sitting on Jo's lap with tongues locked. On seeing this I became very aroused, as this was to be my first viewing of a lesbian experience. While walking the corridors, images of some very sexy and kinky pictures had already taken hold in mind.

I could see, Jo's hands up Ingrid's skirt, as she gently peeled the zipper down, revealing that perfectly rounded ass. Her skin glistened as the evening sunset sky shone through the glass panels on the building. We were on the 18th floor so it was a remarkable site to see.

Ingrid then sat on Jo's desk as Jo gently slipped out of her white cotton dress which I had brought back from my trip to Barbados. Seeing both their bodies in just panties and bras was so appealing to me which was a lot to see but still more to imagine. I remember when growing up, voyeurism was thought to be a taboo and I now understood the reason as this was a powerful and erotic experience.

Their bodies were enter-twined as they kissed and caressed each other. Jo broke the kiss and knelt between Ingrid's thighs spreading her legs and planting them firmly on the table. From my angle Ingrid's pussy's lips were bright pink and the hair on her mound was trimmed in a heart shaped. Jo was licking her pussy like there was no tomorrow and from the sounds and expression of Ingrid, it was quite clear she was almost about to burst. (*As they say a woman knows her body better than a man*). For me standing at the door I has inserted my hand in my pants and had begun to rub my crotch as the feelings became intense just watching these two at it.

Ingrid appeared hungry and insatiable and quickly took hold of Jo while changing positions. She started to lick Jo's nipples which were so erect they stuck out like head beams. I saw the tattoo of the dolphin which was placed in the middle of her breast and this brought a smile to my lips and eyes as during our romps I would have fun playing with it. Just then Ingrid delved between Jo's thighs and made small circular strokes with her tongue. It was like she wanted to explore as she breathed warm air on the lips which seemed to make Jo very responsive. She then used flicking and rubbing movements with her fingers all the while using less pressure as Jo begged for more. Her juices were flowing as she playfully darted a finger into the vagina just as Jo thrust her pelvis forward keeping Ingrid withdrawing for that penetration. Then with one quick motion she thrust three fingers inside giving more intense pleasure.

Before I knew it Jo had pretended to notice me at the door and beckon me in. To my surprise Ingrid wasn't bothered she just kept on. I leaned in and planted a kiss on Jo's lips and Ingrid with one hand grabbed my crotch which was bulged and throbbing.

I quickly slid out of my pants leaving only my shirt unbuttoned with my silk tie dangling on my chest. Ingrid grabbed hold of my cock and placed her lips firmly around the head and using small teasing circles had me groaning, as I French kissed Jo while playing with her pussy with my fingers I had the first taste of Ingrid's juices. She was soaked and needed stuffing, but first I twisted my body and leaned down probing into her vagina with my tongue, then with soft gentle pressure all over her vulva, letting my tongue 'dance'. I remembered something I read and using light flicking rhythmic movements across her clitoris I induced a powerful orgasm from her as she squirted juices into my mouth. I had touched the jackpot—her G-spot (according to Ernst Grafenberg who discovered it) this is said to be found half way up the front wall of the vagina.

I wanted to taste her and so I grabbed her by the hand and sat her on the table and as she spread her legs exposing her pussy and her clit exposed now to me beckoning me to bite. She behaved wildly when I stuck my tongue into her and grabbed hold of my head pulling me into her and screamed, which even made my cock bigger. Jo was grabbing hold of my cock and massaging me and just as Ingrid was about to orgasm pull my cock from Jo's mouth and stuck it into her from that sitting position on the desk, a position similar to the wall thrust I used on her in the photocopier room as I grabbed her hips while she wrapped her legs around me. Her vagina walls were so warm and this position allowed for the blood to be needed elsewhere putting me in control of the pleasure and build up making my orgasm more intense.

I was in this position for a while before I turned her over from the back, to expose her tattoo of a series of stars in procession with some small hearts, which looked beautifully on her back. Her ass was so huge but I grabbed hold of it firmly and slammed every inch of my thick hard cock into her. She then came once again and pushed that enormous ass into me.

Jo was feeling a bit left out so we tried the (upside down position, similar to pan cart) while Ingrid lay on the blue office floor carpet. The material was so soft and she had a magnificent Egyptian rug next to the sofa. The upside-down position Jo had jumped into my arms wrapping her legs around me then letting her body fall backwards into a handstand position with palms on floor as she was then now licking Ingrid's pussy. This position was well impressive and allowed for the pressure to build up in the face, thus producing startling sensations for her during her orgasms. Jo loved new and exciting stuff.

We then changed and I placed her in doggie position which was her favourite thus still allowing her to continue teasing and stimulating Ingrid. Jo produced the most juices I had ever seen from her pussy and with each thrust sounded so good. Then a few minutes I was about to come and they both wanted to taste it all. As I slid out of her they both came like hungry cats for milk, and I spouted my spunk over both of them which they then licked off each other. That was the perfect ending to a week at work.

ESCAPE FROM BRONZE GARDEN

The year was February 6th 2022, and it was broadcasted over the CBN 18:00hrs news that John Carr had escaped.

John at 28 yrs stood tall at 6ft 2 inches of muscular built with a glint of devil and basket full of boyish charm. He had been placed on death row for the Christmas Eve murder of Chris Jack in 2016. John had gone to a club near Euston to celebrate with his mates and during this period he was attacked, and a brawl then ensued. Chris had apparently lunged at John who protected himself but in the heat of the moment with the adrenaline kicking in flew into a drunken rage and pulverised Chris as he fell to the floor. John just kept punching Chris in his head even as the blood flowed onto the floor. This was a very controversial case that had lots of media publicity as John was from a very wealthy prestigious family. He was convicted in September 2017, and placed on Death Row.

While incarcerated he would receive tons of fan mail from women confessing their love and adoration for him. As a young man and knowing that at anytime his life could end, he would daily ask if he can have conjugal visits as his last wish would be to make passionate love to someone. In Prison the female wardens would constantly tease him and taunt him. Bronze Garden was done in a futuristic setting with cameras and alarm pin point settings all over and staff would carry these telecom watches. The walls were extremely high with razor sharp wire all around and lasers which were activated at night with movement sensors. To get into this prison was a nightmare and for a prisoner to get out worse than a nightmare.

On this day, John was supposed to be transported to hospital for a routine follow-up after he had been suffering from severe abdominal pain during the past 7 days. His escape from this trip was well planned and executed with precision. It was reported that on their way to hospital the tires blew out and he then made his escape with the help of three armed men who had bombarded the now toppled van with tear gas. This all happen in a matter of minutes.

It was now about three hours since his escape and information from his fellow inmates was very vague about the circumstances. While he was in prison he used to be visited by a few ladies but there was one particular one with whom he appeared to share a closer bond. Charmaine was a petite lady with a very sex figure, long black shoulder length hair and a neat waist line. Big curvy hips and a large booty to go with it all were the envy of quite a few women she knew. She also had some of the most stunning green eyes and she would smile very seductively as she walk.

John arrived at Charmaine who met him at the door of the Las Plazas Hotel. This was a rundown building in a small quiet town about 80 miles from Bronze Garden with a population of 3,500 where all the people kept to themselves. John had every intention of returning to prison to fulfil his sentence but wanted to enjoy his pleasures before his anticipated execution. On meeting Charmaine, she sprung into his arms and they held each other in a tight embrace with lips locked into each other. Charmaine had intentions to fulfil her man's every fantasy and go out on a limb with him today and give him the time of his life. They both settled onto the settee where she had a meal of two steak romps, baked potatoes, salad and ice cream set out for him. Quite like the last meal of a man on death row, John devoured everything but the ice cream for which he had other plans.

After eating they finish eating, Charmaine rose and went to the kitchen to wash the dishes with john following her shortly afterwards. On approaching she was wearing a short multi-coloured skirt which he quickly threw onto her back as she stood by the sink. Charmaine felt him and immediately spread eagle her legs as he drop down onto floor directly beneath and between her legs, gently pulling her white laced panty apart, thereby exposing her pink labia's, which he quickly clasped his mouth onto.

She grabbed hold of the kitchen tap just as he darted his tongue between her pussy lips, as she moaned and quickly turned the tap off. To give John better leverage she lifted her right leg up onto cupboard, giving him greater advantage and as he parted those lips with his fingers hungrily, he bit and pulled on her pussy causing her juices to flow and drip into his mouth.

Being on the run and with the anticipation and expectation of having Charmaine, John's passion had built up and eagerly he wanted to 'fuck' her gushing honey pot. He rose dropping his pants exposing his now erect eight inches of cock and slid it into Charmaine from behind. She grabbed hold of that kitchen tap with such force that it immediately bent as he plunged his huge promontory deep inside her. He was slamming into her with so much force and pent up longing like a hungry animal devouring its food while she put overlooked the pain and took the eight rock hard inches of cock. After a few minutes John shot his semen into her. Charmaine's pussy was now swollen from his massive cock as they both shuffled into the shower.

In less than five minutes John was ready to have a real go at her sweet, dripping, pussy, and as he lifted Charmaine up to sit on his cock to feel the warm water trickled between them. He was highly pumped and extremely aroused for the occasion as he was bouncing her up and down on him. Resting her onto bathroom wall Charmaine braced her legs onto the rail and took him deep inside her. He was pounding her vigorously as he sucked on her boobs which were so erect and firm and had his name tattooed on them. John was in heaven and couldn't care less about what happened now. Charmaine quickly orgasm and screamed so loudly digging her nails into his shoulder as she held on, this was her second orgasm while in the bathroom as his strokes sent heat waves through her. Her pussy was now well pounded and she mumbled, "I have never felt nor had it like this before".

John was far from orgasm and lifted her out the shower and into the bedroom and placed her onto the bed. He wanted to get all filthy with her and Charmaine likewise, so she slid off his cock and grabbed it with both hands admiring the length and girth before stuffing it into her mouth. Trying to take all in made her gag. She was all about making every moment count for John and she sucked on his shaft making him scream as he shot a load of cum into her hungry mouth. She looked up at him as she swallowed every last drop. John was pleased and dropped onto bed and cuddles Charmaine and kissed her passionately, thanking her for a pleasurable time.

They both laid there for a while watching a rerun of, "The Good, the bad and the ugly", before dozing off. John was however awaken by a highly aroused Charmaine who woke 30 minutes before him and was playing with her swollen pussy and sucking on john's cock, which by now was ready and massively swollen for the events ahead. Charmaine spun around now as she was hyped up and very alert and quickly sat on his face to allow him to eat her as she wanted to suck his 'dick'. John thought to himself that this was the perfect meal. Her pussy was so swollen from his huge manhood but this didn't stop her.

Charmaine now sat placing John's cock into her throbbing pussy and began to bounce trapping his hands onto the bed. As her rhythm got faster, she raised, exposing the tip of his now sensitive cock and plunging down once again until she was about to cum.

She knelt over the bed in doggy style, placing one foot up across mattress and as John entered her from behind she screamed and gritted her teeth as he kept slamming his erect cock in and out of her, until she could take it no longer and begged John to fuck her in the Ass. John had never done anal sex before but at a time like this he didn't care what happened and took his cock and placed it by the entrance. As Charmaine sensed it she backed slowly onto him until it was now part way.

Charmaine had done anal before and told John, "she loved it", her ass was tight and John had to along with her pussy juices find some lubrication. He then began to build momentum and spanked her ass until each cheek was now reddened. All this time Charmaine was playing with her clit until she came several times. John grabbed her hair as he pumped her, arching her back, she took his eight inches in her ass until he shot his load of cum deep within the cavity of her ass. Charmaine then pushed this out onto the floor. Both now exhausted flopped onto the bed and slept until morning.

This was a day to remember but as the prospect of returning to prison could be only a few moments away, John had some other fantasies or last meals to partake of as he says to himself with a smile, this next one will be treated as my last request.

9 781477 213957